Kathleen's Cariole Ride

A True Love Story from over the Ocean and in the Bush

after World War One

Margaret Kell Virany

More authentic photographs and a change of sub-title theme bring
the love story from <u>A Book of Kells: Growing Up in an Ego Void</u>
to a new generation of readers

Dedicated to Each One of You

©Copyright 2014 Margaret Kell Virany, Gatineau, Québec

ISBN 978-0-9699142-5-9
AMICUS No. 43185410
Monograph

NAME(S):*Virany, Margaret Kell author
TITLE(S): Kathleen's cariole ride : a true love story from
over the ocean and in the bush after World War one /

NUMBERS: ISBN: 9780969914259
CLASSIFICATION: LC Class no.: FC27*
Dewey: 920.72/0971 23

V

Virany & Virany Publishing
478 Du Caveau Street
Gatineau, QC J9H 5N7
editingexcellence.virany98@gmail.com

Table of Contents

Kathleen wore a pigtail, played ball sports fiercely and was head of her class

Prologue

Back in the roaring, inventive, optimistic 1920's, an unusual romance developed. An invitation to come to tea offered during the horrific conflagration called World War 1 was followed up almost a decade later by a letter.

Kathleen Elizabeth Ward and John Ambrose Campbell Kell (Jack) were an unlikely pair. Her father was a city councilor in Portsmouth, England (pop. 190,000). His was a farmer in Cookstown, ON, Canada (pop. 550, not counting the cows, horses and pigs).

This story recounts in their words how she was persuaded to leave her country, friends, job, family and everyone she ever knew to follow a colonial sailor to an aboriginal reserve in far northern Manitoba.

Kathleen couldn't have been happier than she was on a sunny August afternoon in 1914. She was playing tennis on the grass court in her garden with her friend, René, and René's older brother Victor. Suddenly their game was interrupted by a radio bulletin declaring that war had broken out on the continent.

The citizenry of Portsmouth turned from being enthusiastic flag-wavers at ceremonial reviews of the fleet into being frightened prey cringing from the shadow of German Zeppelin airships. They darkened their bedroom windows, threatening them with danger from the skies for the first time in their lives.

Kathleen and Victor's dreams of one day marrying each other and having children ended abruptly with his signing up and her going after school to do volunteer sewing at a school converted into a hospital for wounded soldiers.

In France, Victor contracted typhoid fever on the battlefield, was borne home on a stretcher and died at age nineteen. When this brutal blow struck, Kathleen was submerged in grief and vowed to become a doctor so she could help save others.

Jack was boarding at a family friend's in Barrie, Canada for his last year at high school when the war broke out. All male students formed a cadet corps which marched to the railway station to see "the boys" (including their favorite teacher) off. Jack signed up but his father John made him stay and work on their 100-acre farm until he turned nineteen. Then he and his best pals Bill Orchard and Ezra Parkhouse took a train to Toronto and enlisted in the Royal Navy Canadian Volunteer Reserve (RNCVR.) News of fatalities was pouring in, their teacher had been killed and farmers were exempt. But it was the sporting, patriotic, manly, idealistic thing to do. . . not to mention the thrill of marching bands, a sweetheart's farewell kiss, a uniform, pay and free passage to Europe.

The true events of this story take place over the Atlantic Ocean and on the Swampy Cree Indian reserve at Oxford House, Manitoba. World War I is over; the Great Depression and World War II lie ahead. It was an era of inventions, extremes and change as the world became smaller. The automobile and the airplane had arrived. Radio, telephone and telegraph still seemed miraculous. In the United States, buying and selling alcoholic beverages were prohibited. Air ace Charles Lindbergh and the dashing Prince of

Wales were idols. Women got the right to vote and had their long hair cut into short bobs.

Having read the same books was one thing Kathleen and Jack had in common. They understood how knights and ladies behave, are tried and deceived, stick to their vows, rescue each other when they get into trouble and finally triumph. They devoted their lives to regaining balance and making the world a better place. 'Texting' in those days meant living by a text from the Bible.

When I was a child, I thought my parents' bedroom with two bear skins on the floor, complete with heads, eyes, open jaws, teeth and claws, was a strange place to seek comfort. But they loved incongruity and had fond memories of the north and the aftermath of the war. The spark of love that was ignited while a brutal conflict raged developed into an eternal flame in Canada's snowy expanses and deep-frozen lakes.

Near the end of her cariole ride of a life, Kathleen left a sheaf of love letters locked in a keepsake box by the wayside, hoping a faithful scribe might come by and pass her story along to a fellow adventurer.

As Jack left for war his father said, "I won't see you again."

1. Faltering at Falling in Love

After they finished training on the *HMS Niobe* in Halifax, Jack and his buddies were posted to Portsmouth, England. A sign on a telephone pole outside the barracks (where they were learning how to swim, among other things) invited colonial servicemen to come to the Young Men's Bible Class at Wesley Methodist Chapel. Afterwards the teacher Walter Ward invited them to his home to have tea with his wife Elizabeth, eldest daughter Kathleen and twins Enid and Eric.

Jack survived one and one-half years as a gunner on a trawler in the North Sea and English Channel, sweeping for mines and sinking German U boats. His father died after his lung was punctured by a sharp branch in a fall from an apple tree and infection set in. Jack bonded with the kind Mr. Ward who invited him to his home a few more times and Enid, the more outgoing daughter, started writing to him after he was redeployed to Halifax. Depressed by the ruthless killing and inhumanity he had seen, he wrote in his 1918 diary on his 21st birthday, "Now I know I am a failure." Just after the Armistice was signed Ernie Taylor, a YMCA war service secretary, told Jack sailors were needed for an expedition to escort the Canadian warship *Stadacona* through the Panama Canal from Halifax to Victoria, so off they adventured to exotic ports. After being discharged Jack went on to get a higher education as his father's will stipulated.

He graduated from Victoria College, University of Toronto, was chosen Senior Stick (an all-round award), and took a summer job with the Methodist Church of Canada at Warren's Landing, a fishing village at the tip of Lake Winnipeg. When he saw prospectors, trappers, teachers, missionaries, nurses, etc. get off the steamboat and keep going north he decided not to return south in the fall as planned.

The British Methodists wanted to evangelize the aboriginals and the Canadian government wanted to bring them into a more homogeneous Canada. Jack signed on for a job to start a teaching and preaching mission at God's Lake, a Swampy Cree settlement (pop. 328). It was thought that education would help loosen traditional ties that might foment unrest and threaten stability. It would be difficult but Jack had faith the people would choose to progress. He hoped they'd follow the white man's virtues, rather than his vices.

With a year's supplies purchased in Winnipeg, he steamed up to Norway House where his supervisor Rev. Samuel (Papa) Gaudin and his wife Anna, RN greeted him. Jack got instructions and medical supplies from the doctor, bought a Cree dictionary, packed his canoe and waited. God's Lake could be reached in six days by those willing and able to portage twenty times, shoulder their way through narrow bush trails, scramble on all fours over high rocks, and slog through foot-deep *muskeg* (swamp).

After four days two Cree guides, one of them a WWI vet, came. Soon Jack was being wafted into the unknown, camping at night with a group who taught him how they worshipped and asked him to lead in praying and singing. For five days the paddles dipped

10

into silent, lonely, mirror-like lakes, clear to the bottom, reflecting exquisite northern landscapes and sky.

At last the setting sun illumined a scene of human misery with red, purple, pink, mauve, yellow and green pastels. Five or six houses stood amid rotting trees, abandoned shacks and scores of thin, sniffing, howling dogs. As the canoe approached the people cried out, "The *ayumahaogimow* (praying boss) is here!" A good man had come to help them gain access to the world of dreams and *manitous* (gods) and exercise control over the *wetigoes* (evil spirits) through praying and hymn-singing.

Next day, twelve miles farther up at God's Narrows, Jack landed in a crowd of wedding guests celebrating the chief's daughter's marriage with drumming, dancing and feasting. They would have gone on all night if the elders hadn't quieted them for an outdoor service. Jack strung up his Navy hammock in a fish hut vacated by a departing government agent who gave him a list of indigent families he was to distribute supplies to monthly.

While he waited three weeks for a man to drag his bags through the *muskeg* all the way from the Echimamish (flowing both ways) River, he observed aboriginal life. The Cree were generous, good-looking, jovial, proud, clever people who put out fishing nets that quickly filled with jackfish, whitefish, pickerel, trout and suckers. It wasn't as easy as it looked but Jack had to learn how to do it in order to survive. The women snared small animals like rabbit and mink, while the men hunted big game like moose, bear, wolf and deer.

11

Jack was no weakling but he couldn't match the Cree in speed, strength and endurance. On a 20-mile run through the bush to see if anyone living in an isolated shack needed help, he came upon Donald Ross who was laid up with sore feet. The only thing Jack could think of doing was to coat them with mustard and soak them in warm water. When Donald recovered, he gave Jack some meat and a pair of moccasins so he could run faster.

The Cree resented that the power they had wielded in a Golden Age when the hunt was plentiful had been usurped. The Government deemed them to be self-governing and self- sufficient but it wasn't so. Jack thought it did no good to dwell on what it was like before the white man came. Who would want to go back to the days of having no matches, tomahawks, rifles, metal axes, stoves, kettles, pots, pans, embroidery silks, beads and needles? He felt the Church and Government had behaved generously towards the aboriginal people. Encroachers or epidemics would have killed them if they hadn't signed treaties to create reserves with exclusive hunting rights and other provisions. The Cree said white men had misused their women. Tuberculosis and the effects of VD were killing the very young. Eighty-five out of 100 deaths on the reserve were of people under age sixty. Jack hoped to set an example of better behavior.

He claimed seventy-five acres on a hill across the Narrows from the Hudson Bay Company (HBC) post to build a log house. He bought an ax, chopped down trees, sawed logs, and jumped each time one of the people popped out from behind a tree to watch him.

When they saw how hard he worked, they volunteered one by one to help. It started to snow as they put moss on the roof, covered it with thin poles and tar paper and chinked the walls with mud, made by softening earth over a bonfire. Then Jack banked up the foundation with moss, brush and snow, installed a door, window and stove and built a "parliament building" (Cookstown humor for outhouse.)

Dulas McIvor, the HBC factor, gave him old boxes to use for flooring. He was the son of a Scottish trader and a Cree woman; his wife Alice was a graduate of the residential school in Norway House. Jack bought a rifle from them and occasionally shot rabbits for dinner.

According to the tribe's ancient beliefs, Jack had claimed a holy place, the second highest hill along the old fur trade route from Norway House to York Factory. It was inhabited by the progenitor of all otters who had transmitted special healing powers to a medicine man. God's Lake was named for the *manitous* animating natural objects, such as a lake teeming with fish and an odd-shaped rock.

In mid-October, the log shack was finished and forty-six people in thirteen canoes came to the first indoor church service. Only one pupil attended the first day of school so Jack made the rounds to sell the idea of education. He sat on a box inside the flap-door of Tom Duck's animal-skin teepee and watched fish for winter dog food being smoked on a dozen poles around a fire which vented itself through a hole at the top. The elders and a married son with his wife and children stood on one side; unmarried family members on the other.

Jack knew his sales pitch had succeeded when Donald, Katie and Hattie Trout turned up for school. Soon twelve children were studying basic reading, writing and arithmetic. They learned to tell the time, use a calendar and observe a strange custom, Halloween, in which Jack broke his flashlight and cut his hand doing a shadow trick. The children helped him pick up words in Cree, a melodious language.

After introducing the Nativity story, Jack went by dog team to Oxford House to get presents, ice cream and a Santa Claus suit for a Christmas concert. When he came back on a toboggan pulled by a horse (*mistatim*, meaning big dog) some folks ran and hid.

After his supplies arrived and he learned how to bake bread, Jack invited the McIvors for dinner and they invited him back. When he shopped at their store he picked up the latest gossip: Jimmy, the

14

clerk, caught an ermine and Alice received a mink in payment for food. This social life was cut off when, to get to see them, Jack had to throw a rope across the channel, cling to it as he walked fifteen feet, then paddle in the canoe, then walk over ice for 100 yards. Nothing could get in or out of the reserve as the season changed and the ice thickened. Then several dog teams came and Jack sent out twenty letters. The temperature plunged; the children stayed home. Cold, hunger and toothaches set in but were not as hard to bear as the isolation and loneliness of a God's Lake winter.

Jack had no radio and seldom anyone to talk to in English. He read novels by Sir Walter Scott and Charles Dickens, recorded his observations of Cree family structures and social customs, built a table and wrote sermons that Dulas delivered in Cree. One night the chief came to the door to say his mother had died. After the funeral, eight dogs pulled her on a *cariole* (big toboggan used for special occasions and as a hearse) to her resting-place in the cemetery.

On a visit to the Trout/Duck family in their winter shack, Jack had to get past a dozen starving dogs and pups in the doorway. Large quarters of frozen moose meat from a hunt were lying on the roof so now the family and dogs would be happy. Twelve people lived in the 12' by 15' shack with no floor, partitions or beds. They slept fanned out on spruce boughs with their feet to the fire and their heads to the outer rim. A huge kettle was boiling on the stove but Jack declined to stay for supper. He didn't want to run the risk that, in a day or two, they'd all be sick by auto-suggestion and blame him for it. Most of the Cree lived in fear of other people's dream gods, thinking they got sick or unlucky only if someone wanted them to.

While Jack was lonely, the Cree had Wesukechak, the embittered, flattering one of ancient oral Cree legend, to keep them company. This hungry, wandering trickster and superhuman hero could talk to the birds, animals and spirits—even the Kitche Manitou (Great Spirit.) The people knew Wesukechak had never really existed, yet he kept them together. He was just like they were; he was the spirit of the Cree. A Wesukechak story explained everything from how the world was created to why the loon's back was flat. The hero was tricked, got into fights, got warts on his face and had to solve riddles to find love. The elders embellished the stories as they told them at night around the winter fire. The people kept these intimate, often sexy, myths to themselves because they had been told they were heathen. Jack knew they were more than fairy tales; they were a way of telling a society what it needed to know in order to survive.

On his first solo dog team trip, Jack's home-made sleigh fell apart and his dogs ran away so he had to borrow more. In February, guides took him sixty miles to Island Lake, a settlement of 625 aboriginal people, to compare notes with the teacher, Miss Sturdy. On their way they passed Young Lady Lake (three rivals fought for her, two of them killing each other), Wesukechak's Seat (a split rock), Wesukechak's Spoon (a spoon-shaped rock) and the Lake of Dancing with Your Eyes Shut. At this last spot, Wesukechak invited all the birds—grouse, ptarmigan, goose, duck, kingfisher, bittern,

16

sapsucker, owl, gull, robin, eagle, marten, partridge, chickadee, whiskeyjack, woodpecker, raven, swallow, fisher, osprey, prairie chicken, hawk and meadowlark—for a dance. He told them to close their eyes and then he wrung the duck's neck so he could have a meal.

When his year's contract ended, Jack reported to the Gaudins in Norway House and fell head over heels in love at the first sight of their 15-year-old daughter Esther. It was totally inappropriate for him to have such feelings for a girl eleven years younger than he was. Summoning all the resources he had to resist temptation and not stray from the correct path for his life, he buried his forbidden love inside and turned tail. To save his soul and his career, he fled south to the security of Victoria College and an MA program in history.

He wanted to salvage something optimistic from this hard experience in the north so, before leaving, Jack bought two bear skins, one black and one white. He clung to his faith that one day he would have a wife and a home which might be in need of the odd, splendid accoutrement, such as bedside rugs for cold feet.

Kathleen came up with an almost giddy idea for a double's game of tennis.

2. Tennis Torture

Meanwhile on the other side of the ocean, Kathleen was accepted into the London School of Medicine for Women but stayed in high school to study sciences for an extra year, which was a bad one. She became exhausted, caught the Spanish flu followed by a series of colds and barely dragged herself to the Armistice celebration on Nov.11, 1918. Another girl was chosen "most popular" in an open vote and her idol Lois didn't write to her while studying at Oxford University. A young man from the Sunday school proposed to her but she turned him down because she did not love him enough and had five years of heavy studies ahead of her. He was terribly upset and neither of them slept for nights.

To recuperate, she went to the Lakes district with a friend whose sister was married to a clergyman. But Kathleen's nerves just got worse. She felt acrophobic while climbing up a slippery mountain and was horrified when a sudden storm came up and two people drowned in a nearby lake. Then she had to baby-sit with her hosts' toddler and help them pack when they got word they were being moved to another parish. She felt tired out when she got back home and had to get ready to leave her family for the first time in her life.

Elizabeth, Enid and Eric accompanied her on the train to London and installed her at the home of relatives with ten days to relax, so they thought, but her two cousins suddenly had to have their tonsils out and Auntie Lily came down with an abscessed foot. Kathleen, who had never even boiled a potato, had to cook for Uncle

Frank and run the household. Then, the night before the term started, all England's trains, even London's underground tube, went on strike.

Kathleen loved the campus atmosphere and medical studies but the cross-town commute was nerve-wracking as the strike continued. One day she tried to board a moving bus and would have been dragged under if other passengers had not grabbed her and lifted her up. Another day she thought she could walk the last part of the way home but got hopelessly lost.

Suddenly, her nerves crocked completely and she could not go on. Walter came to get her and a woman doctor in Portsmouth prescribed pills and diagnosed her problem as *psychasthenia*, literally a weakness of the spirit or soul. She had very little nervous stamina and would never be able to lead the life of a doctor. She must take a complete rest and always watch herself to make sure she did not get overtired. Kathleen faced up to reality and quit medical school. She had hoped to do well and please her parents but didn't want to waste their money.

She soothed her nerves by reading everything from cheap pamphlets to leather-bound works by the Romantic and Victorian poets and novelists. She stared out over the sea from the Isle of Wight, kept a commonplace book of poems and scraps of wisdom, attended church and helped her mother with charitable works. When well enough, she took up dressmaking, needlepoint, cooking, typing and book-keeping at the municipal college. When better yet, she enrolled in a degree program in mathematics, English and history and took part in a suffragette demonstration. After three years of study, she quit university just before the final exams after rejecting another suitor.

The J.B. Ward & Sons bakery opened a café above a shop at a downtown intersection around this time and Walter hired Kathleen to manage it. This work suited her to a tee. She hired, fired, supervised, ordered food, planned and wrote out menus, served customers, took in cash, kept the books, had the walls repainted and was the gossip center for friends and family. This was not what she had expected to do with her life, but she also led a club for ten- to twelve-year-old girls from the slums and sang in the philharmonic choir and at fundraisers. She planned to work for Eric who was setting up a law office. She did not expect to marry because so few eligible men had survived the war (in fact, 886,342 English men had been killed in action). All attempts to match her up with someone had fizzled. She disliked the Varsity snobs she met at tennis parties and dances.

In early December, 1924 Enid married an Australian sailor, Joseph Burnett, whose ship was being refitted in the Portsmouth dockyards. They honeymooned in Switzerland and got back to find out Joe had been put in charge of the crew of twenty-five who would be on duty over Christmas. The question was, how would he round the sailors up and get them back on board after spending their leave wallowing in debauchery around the harbor? They'd all be drunk.

When Elizabeth and Walter got wind of this, they invited the whole crew to come and celebrate Christmas with them. They prepared the food in Grandfather Ward's house, while a party complete with his stories of diamond-mining in South Africa, Eric's conjuring tricks, ukuleles, cocked hats, raunchy Australian songs and recitations rocked their own house next door. Even Grandfather Wooller and his maiden daughters had fun. But, at the end of the day, the sailors left and Kathleen was still alone. Then came May, when Enid sailed away to her new life in Australia.

The world hath no creativity like that of a woman resisting the fate of spinsterhood and Kathleen had an idea. In a thorough way, she went through the correspondence Enid had been taking care of on behalf of the family and was now abandoning. One of the three Canadian sailors she'd been writing to ever since they came to their home for tea in 1917 was evidently not married and was studying in Toronto. Kathleen had met students from Victoria College at an international conference, where a speaker on sex had said it should be an expression of the entire personality. If she ever found the right man, she would devote herself to him completely, as well as to a higher cause. Nothing in the courtly love convention prevented the lady from lighting a candle to beckon from her tower window so she sat down in her upstairs office at the café and picked up a pen.

Picture Jack as he stood on the roof of Victoria College to watch the eclipse of the moon on New Year's Eve. He was beginning to savor success. He was finishing his MA in history under Lester Bowles Pearson who was to become Prime Minister of Canada some forty years later. Jack sometimes went out with his sister, Clara, who was also alone in the city, or took a co-ed to the theater or skating. Methodists didn't dance. He worked part-time as student minister at a three-point rural charge, had invested in three building lots, and bought a bootlegger's Touring car for $200 at an auction. All he needed to do was complete a one-year degree in theology at Emmanuel College and find a wife.

But when he got back down to earth things didn't go so well. He and his high school sweetheart, Suzy, had grown apart after he came home from WWI but it still hurt when she married someone else. He proposed to another girl but she broke off their engagement when she found out he wanted to go up north to an aboriginal reserve. He had won the preaching prize at college but rejected a job at the huge Metropolitan Methodist Church in the city. He was the best man twice for close friends and wished it was his turn to be the groom.

Just as he was running out of co-eds to date, Kathleen's letter arrived out of the blue. How well he remembered Walter Ward's lovely eldest daughter who was not as outgoing as her younger sister. He had surmised that she was already taken. He could not romance her yet, that would not be polite, but Canada and the United Church could.

He replied with knightly courtesy, inquiring if it were not Portsmouth that had the most beautiful women managing its cafés. He admired her business acumen, of which he had none. Theology was his line and he worked on the side as a simple country curate for three small congregations. They were kind folk who teased him about the way he held a baby for baptism. He happened to have a car

23

and would be present at the founding of the United Church of Canada, an event that was attracting international attention.

Ignoring the flirtatiousness, Kathleen maintained the cover of good family friend, passing on the Wards' news and inquiring about life in Canada. Her family had moved away from New Road, where he had visited them, and were making *The Cottage* in Waterlooville their permanent home. Soon they would be getting electric light. She enclosed a picture of their grass tennis court and said she was looking forward to playing.

Jack replied that baseball was all the rage here but, if he were a decent tennis player, he would offer to play her a game. Since she had asked about life on this side of the ocean, he said the English were behind the Canadians in agricultural methods but not in much else. Some "Old Country misfits" grumbled a lot and the hardier Cookstown villagers felt like telling them to go back home.

The uniting of three of Canada's major Protestant denominations in Mutual Street Arena on June 10, 1925 made one-third of the Canadian church-going population into an organic whole. Banner headlines, visiting Church dignitaries, a crowd of 24,000 in three sittings and a record heat wave made it a heady international event. A wind orchestra played, communion was served and the Mendelssohn Choir led in singing hymns and the Catholic creed. The night before, 8,641 out of 9,433 Congregationalist, Methodist, Presbyterian and Local Union congregations had cast final ballots to unite after twenty-five years of lobbying and $175,000 in legal fees. A feeling of pioneering spiritual adventure surged and tolerance, peace and social justice were thought to be just around the corner. Jack was there and experienced the "enjoyment, belonging, consummation, spirit, beauty and impressiveness" of the occasion.

The exchange of courteous letters continued until Kathleen got wound up in the holiday round of work, festivities and balls and let the correspondence lapse. Jack waited for the lady to take her turn and, when she finally did, he was not about to let her get away again. He told her he would be one of the first thirteen ministers ordained in the new Church and planned to go north to do Indian mission work for five or six years.

Then his fountain pen splurged out of control and took on a life of its own, suggesting that she also had a sense of adventure and might want to throw in her lot with his. He said he had always secretly hoped that she, not Enid, would be the one to write and had dropped rather broad hints to that effect. As soon as he mailed this letter, he wanted it back. He wrote again. He hadn't said anything about love because he didn't know whether she was free. He told her he had had a girlfriend at the time he met her, and another one since then, but was now just a carefree youth.

Kathleen sent back a carefully reasoned answer, feigning surprise. She had always liked him but never thought of him as anything other than a good, close, family friend. However, since they were now writing to each other on this level, it would be best if he could come over for a visit. They had not seen each other for nine years and then only a few times. She was perfectly free, although two men had wanted her but she rejected them. Their letters got through in spite of the general strike of workers in England.

Jack could squeeze in a trip to England before his job at Oxford House, northern Manitoba started and secretly hoped to get engaged now and marry next year. To pay for passage, he sold his car to his brother, Wilson, and taught him how to drive so he could get back home. Jack sent Kathleen his picture so she would not be expecting to see a 20-year-old sailor.

Walter met Jack in Southampton and brought him to *The Cottage*, where Kathleen and Elizabeth were ostensibly relaxing in the garden with a cigarette and a cocktail. Thoughts of the Prohibition petition he had just signed, and all else, fled Jack's mind as he looked into the pair of sea-blue eyes he had never forgotten. He was completely overcome by feelings of tenderness, protectiveness and love and was struck dumb. Fortunately, she was a good conversationalist. The girl of his dreams had not changed, even if the school uniform was gone and the long brunette pigtail anchored at the nape of the neck with a huge bow had been replaced by a fashionable flapper's bob.

Kathleen regretted that he could stay for only six days. They walked, talked, played tennis, met friends, looked at Eric's law office and saw a play. Walter invited Jack to lunch with Lord Askwith, guest speaker at a Portsmouth Brotherhood meeting of 1500 men that night where Jack was to read the scripture. This non-church, non-political organization gave homecoming servicemen a place to go to keep up their morale. Organized religion was being rebuffed but impulses for human betterment had survived the war.

Kathleen was finding Jack very different from the other young men she knew. The clock was ticking and she had only two days to make the most momentous decision of her life. He could see she was getting tense and felt sorry his presence affected such a dear, intelligent, genuine, sweet creature this way. On the fourth day, she told him she was very fond of him and enjoyed his company but couldn't possibly marry him. It would be too risky.

The whole household tossed and turned that night. Jack felt more miserable than at any other time in his life. Elizabeth found her daughter's behavior reprehensible and felt sorry for him. Kathleen was a nervous wreck. Walter was convinced his daughter was making a terrible mistake. In the morning, Elizabeth, Eric and Jack had an uncomfortable breakfast together. Then he went downtown alone but Walter retrieved him and took him to a Rotary Club dinner at noon.

In the evening, Kathleen came up with an almost giddy idea for a double's game of tennis, the men against the women. Walter was an excellent player, capable of secretly throwing a game in order not to embarrass a guest. Jack had played only a little in Cookstown and at college. Elizabeth had played all her life. On this occasion Kathleen was absolutely smashing, her lithe figure bending, stretching and running down every ball. She outmaneuvered even Walter and the women won. Jack's grace in losing was the prelude to his departure from the theater of England.

27

Kathleen watches a ship sail off from Southampton on a dreary day

3.   Left Hanging over 5,000 Miles of Fog and Bog

I couldn't imagine my parents had ever been attractive or in love; they were just dutifully, decently bound to each other. But I saw them differently after a day in 1996 when I turned the key in the lock of my mother's metal keepsake box and let loose seventy-two flimsy, hand-written letters which had logged 200,000 miles between historic Portsmouth, England and a Canadian Indian reserve.

The tennis game they played in 1926 was just the opening volley in a lifelong game of love. Kathleen was elated by the feminist victory on the court and, next day, she and Jack toured the Isle of Wight with Elizabeth and Aunt Alice in a char-a-banc (a cross between a limousine and a hay wagon.) Jack was put back behind the baseline of trusted family friend while they ate lunch tête à tête in a hotel garden. Kathleen even treated him to the family's blackly humorous riddle: The Wards had emigrated from France long ago and set up a farm near Shanklin on the Isle of Wight, where they had twenty-one children twice. (First they had twenty-one but one died. Then they had another one.)

The next day Kathleen accompanied Jack to the Port of Southampton as he set sail in the fog and the drear on a lone journey to a mission field 5,000 miles away. Seized by curiosity, she asked if she could board the *Minnedosa* with him to deposit his luggage and see the inside of a transatlantic liner's cabin. Then they browsed in the dockside shops and bought each other a souvenir. She had to leave first, so he settled her on her train with (I'm willing to bet) a farewell kiss and told her he wouldn't give up hope for a year. She said if he met someone else in the meantime she would wish them well. Then she went to the Isle of Wight with some of her cousins to rest her nerves for a fortnight. She stared at the sea, took pictures of the lighthouse in the fog and got an awful sunburn.

Jack had scarcely left when a letter he mailed from Queenstown, Ireland arrived at Ryde. It was cheery in tone: "I haven't yet met any girl I like better than you," he wrote. "Pardon me for having my little joke but I was really wondering if you thought I could do such a thing. I said 'could' not 'would'. By now, the sight of a lady smoking is no more revolting to me than one chewing gum—they all seem to smoke. But give me good old American spearmint any day." Kathleen replied that a play she saw made her more strongly inclined than ever to dislike gum-chewing.

Jack wrote a diary letter of his ocean-crossing. Among the passengers were several war brides who had been to England to show off their children. The book Kathleen had given him, Shepherd Easton's Daughter, had led him to ponder a problem at the crux of his ministry. How could one church appeal both to the practically minded and to the mystically inclined? At Quebec City, 100 steerage passengers disembarked and got on another boat headed for New York City. In Montreal, Jack helped some Dutch passengers find a hotel; he'd been teaching them to speak English during the crossing.

He had to rush on to Richmond Hill to conduct farewell services for his three congregations. Then he went home and sent Kathleen pictures of Cookstown which, "unlike an English country village, is built around four corners where four main roads meet, each of them going to one of the points of the compass. With regard to buildings, it can hold its own." Now that he knew the person at the other end of the letters, he could make efforts to bond. Kathleen had hinted at having had a car accident (she had, in fact, demolished the iron entrance gate at St. Cross Hospital in Winchester.) So, when Jack disgraced himself by driving the family car right through the garage and six feet out the other side, he told her about it. The gas feed, clutch and brake on a McLaughlin were so different from those on a Ford!

As Jack sped westward on the Canadian National Railway's *The National*, he had poor substitutes for the wife he had hoped to have with him to share missionary life. A copy of Gentlemen Prefer Blondes lay on his lap and 19-year-old (actually seventeen but lying about his age) Jim Johnston sat at his side. The book was from college pals who had sprung a surprise farewell party and razzed him about his English girl. Jim was a professor's son who was going up to Oxford House to teach school and would room with Jack. Wires laid alongside the railway tracks carried cabled messages and the miracle of radio enabled them to get news "faster than standing-still people." They wore headsets in the lounge car, while a white-gloved operator manipulated the dials to bring in local stations.

In the dining car, Jack sat opposite a Progressive member of the House of Commons who was fresh from the most raucous session of parliament in the country's history. "It proved very exhilarating," Jack wrote. "He let out a lot of political secrets and quite convinced me that Premier (William Lyon Mackenzie) King is as crooked as a snake." Late into the night, Jack and Jim swayed outside on the dusty caboose.

When they got to Winnipeg, Jim led the search to find just the right radio and finally chose one which cost $105, batteries and all. Shopping at a warehouse for a year's supply of food, clothing and other necessities took less time. They bought a tent, blankets, 12 lbs of dried apples, 12 lbs of prunes, 24 cans of peaches, 24 tins of pineapple, 36 lbs of jam, 60 lbs of honey, 100 lbs of bacon and enough baking powder to keep them in bread and cookies. They would barter the jam and honey with the hunters for fish and meat.

Meanwhile, Kathleen pried open yet-another crate of tomato soup in her café and sat down to take a break. Thinking about what to write to a friend far off in the bush was a creative release. Her day was ten hours long, and often frenetic, but had quiet interludes when she sat in her office or beside the fire. Letters to and from Jack had found a niche in her daily round. She felt his work was important, especially when she read of the loving send-offs his congregations gave him. She needed to let the supportive, frivolous side of her nature come out without making any commitments.

One day, she collapsed laughing after a customer said an egg she served him was not as fresh as it might be and a stand-off ensued. Another day, she copied out so many menus she was sure 'Tomato Soup' would be found written across her heart when she died. Then she turned serious and wrote, "Isn't it absolutely disgusting that food plays such an important part in people's lives? We're all equally dependent on it but we don't have to be equally fond of it." She was repulsed by the over-indulgence she saw at municipal receptions, banquets and balls.

As Kathleen mused, Jack steamed slowly up Lake Winnipeg, checked what time it was on her clock and wrote, "This part of our trip is simply gorgeous with ideal, warm, fresh evenings aboard ship. Canadians, i.e. real native-born Canadians, are always enthusiastic about our weather. Grumbling at the weather is not the popular pastime here that it seems to be in England." Kathleen had to agree that if a customer at the cash asked her for the time of day, instead of complaining about the weather, it was a brilliant effort at conversation.

At Norway House, Jack wrote, "The moon is temptingly beautiful, tempting one not to go to bed. You would be agreeably surprised at the community life of this far northern post. There aren't a great many white people but they are of an exceptionally high caliber." Of the residential school graduation exercises for a class of seven, he said, "The boys are eager and the girls well-mannered. The evolution of these people is a fascinating process, full of disappointments and perplexities, but supremely gratifying in the long run."

As he and Jim left Norway House, fifteen new-found friends sang For They Are Jolly Good Fellows and tossed bananas, biscuits and chocolate bars into their canoe. As they skimmed along, Jack wondered how he could help the spiritual growth of the people. "This is a hard job just because so few want to do it or think it worthwhile but I have faith that, being in my right place, my God whom I try to serve will see me through." He feared he was making himself too important what with being doctor, welfare officer, police magistrate and missionary but it was all in a lifetime. His guide Isaac Mason, a very intelligent Cree elder who took Jack under his wing, traded beans, tea and sugar for freshly killed moose meat when they met a canoe going the opposite way.

After five days of sailing over a multitude of rivers and lakes, they reached an ancient summer camping ground of a semi-nomadic tribe of hunters. This gathering place of the Swampy Cree on the northeastern ridge of Lake Waypinaponipee (water with a deep hole in it) was called Oxford House by the white man. From here the Hayes River flowed into Hudson Bay at York Factory. Jack hoped the chief and his band would interpret the breeze that blew their canoe right up to their feet as a good omen. Many of them were away working in Norway House as transporters or guides. Jack looked down at the rich, black soil and got his first idea of how he could help these happy, hungry folk.

Inside *Mission House*, he placed Kathleen's picture in its Lake Louise souvenir frame on his study desk overlooking a splendid beach. It was July 23, 1926 and this was his birthday celebration. "At last I feel I have stopped running away from you," he wrote.

Jack was finding it was no mean trick to keep a transatlantic courtship going

4. Courting an English Girl While Living in the Bush

Jack's first impression was that some of the people were crude, superstitious and ignorant while others were choice, educated and progressive. One helper, Thomas Noah, preached very well, although Jack couldn't understand a word he was saying. He had had one arm shot off at the shoulder but could paddle a canoe, run rapids, drive dog teams, carry freight, trap and hunt as well as any man. The chief was a fine chap who, while not very musical, played the organ and led the singing. Jack was amazed at how inspired the people looked when Isaac translated his sermons for him. Dulas, who had moved here from God's Lake, told Jack the congregation was getting two sermons: one was his and the other was Isaac's. Some of them understood the humanizing message of a God of love, while others layered it onto their traditional beliefs. It made sense to believe in the white man's god when they were with the white man and in their own gods when they were alone.

Kathleen wondered how her letter got through to a place with no post office. Jack told her it arrived with the treaty party (the doctor and Indian agent) by seaplane. The Government had made the aboriginal people its wards in 1876, when each band surrendered its rights to certain lands in return for sole rights to a reserve the size of one square mile per person. They would get free medical attention, a school, a teacher, food for the old and sick, and a quantity of shot, netting, flour, sugar and tea for each family. Each member, from eldest to newest-born, also got an annuity of $5, with the chief and councilors receiving more.

Kathleen wrote that she had invited forty little girls from the slums to *The Cottage* to see a woods for the first time. They yelled, tugged at her skirt and dived heedlessly into the dense thicket to the point where she panicked. With help, she managed to get everybody back together in a 'crocodile line'. They spent the day having a wildflower-picking contest, playing games and huddling in the dining room for tea when it rained. Then they climbed onto the *char-a-banc* to leave, waving and singing Show Me the Way to Go Home. Jack said they sang the same song on the reserve but, in contrast to Kathleen's wards, the Oxford House girls were shy. They came to his back door with currants and berries but hid around the side of the house until he called '*astum*' (come here) several times. He served fresh raspberries and red currant pie to his guests, and strained boiled raspberries to make wine for communion. Among the customers at

Kathleen's café were a teacher who couldn't get a job and a doctor who was working as a waitress. Jack said some doctors, dentists and engineers in Canada were having trouble finding work too.

The first month on the reserve, Jim suffered from homesickness and chest pains and was taken out to Norway House, so Jack had to teach school. He wrote, "I say to myself, if these people had progressed according to Darwin's principle of evolution, to the place where they would be establishing schools and places of worship, what kind would they be? I think one can sort of graft Christian principles onto their institutions." Recreation was difficult because dance was the children's only social tie, apart from church, and it was hard to regulate. Jim's problems were due to a drastic change in lifestyle and having grown too fast. The doctor scolded him, saying nobody under military age should attempt to live in the north. School attendance leapt from fourteen to twenty-six under Jack's program of English, arithmetic, geography, drawing, conversation, calendar, time-telling, singing and group games.

"I walked through the woods to-day and felt absolutely entranced by the superb color combinations in the leaves," he wrote in September. "There has been a breeze off the lake and a little fire in our dining room has not come amiss. Nature always appeals to me when the wind is bending the trees and white-capped waves roll up on the shore." As winter drew near, he bought Black Beauty, a heifer, from the HBC post. She was about to be put down since no one could afford to feed her. Jack was already looking after Tommy, his predecessor's horse, and he could haul enough hay for both animals.

Meanwhile, Kathleen was pondering whether she could ever leave England or marry a man who wasn't an English gentleman.

The federal election came and went with the reserve four days away from the nearest polling station. It snowed fiercely as the Cree moved out to their winter camps in groups of four or five families. They would live in shacks, shoot ducks and moose, and fish for themselves and their dogs. The children would be more contented and healthy out in the bush with meat to eat. Jack and Jim gave them their scribblers and texts and told their fathers to make sure they spent some time at them each day. The elderly, the mothers with small children, and men who were too sick or injured to hunt stayed behind.

Jack was finding it no mean trick to keep a transatlantic courtship going. An old man who was bringing the freight in from Norway House took sick and left his bundle of supplies and mail destined for Oxford House tied to a tree ninety miles away. Jack sent two men after it. A float-plane dropped down but didn't stay long enough to pick up a letter. After that, Jack resolved always to have one partially written. On October 10th, he was writing about his potato crop when he heard a plane. He rushed out, stuffing the letter inside his waistcoat from whence it disappeared in the snow. Fortunately, the three map-survey photographers stayed overnight, so he wrote another one. They were getting set to leave when he realized this was his chance to send Christmas greetings to the

Wards. He had bought Kathleen a pair of embroidered white deerskin fur-trimmed moccasins made for an Indian princess. As he was running to the plane, he saw the letter he had lost in the snow so sent it too.

Kathleen kept on writing regularly, even if she got no replies. She thought Jack was a real sport for doing what he was doing and wished they could sit down together and have a good old chat. She was reading H.G. Wells' World of William Clissold, while he was reading books on the North American Indian. He believed in offering people constructive ideas without scolding—one of the worst crimes people commit, he felt, well deserving of punishment under the law. Kathleen pleaded "Guilty" and wondered what her sentence would be.

The reserve's only radio picked up concerts each night from New York, Chicago, San Antonio, Los Angeles, Washington, Portland and Seattle. The Zion Broadcasting Station, built and financed by a rich man in Illinois, sent out nightly concerts which came in very distinctly. After seeing a snapshot of Jack, Jim and the Hudson Bay folk sitting spellbound, Kathleen wrote, "You seem to have rapt expressions which might, I suppose, be called radio face." One night Jack was up late, waiting for the bread to bake, when he heard a tenor voice singing Do I Miss You? Deed'n I Do. He wrote, "It's lonesome up here and I'm thinking always of you, wanting you for my companion and inspiration. I would be raised to seventh heavens of joy if you would give me your love. Somehow I feel absolutely safe with you; I never felt the same with anyone else. I

39

feel no barrier whatsoever. All that I have is yours. I know not if this is not for some purpose which lies beyond our ken. I wish we could tune in to one another's thoughts." Silence from Portsmouth.

An urgent knock on the door summoned Jack to go out to the chief's winter camp. He had gone crazy and was terrorizing the people. After getting there as quickly as possible, Jack calmed the chief down and held a service with the people. On the trip home, Jack and Jamesie, his guide, came upon a burly wolf who had two toes caught in a trap and was fighting to get free. Jamesie said they must kill the animal before it chewed off its foot and got loose. They picked up two sticks and hit six swift blows to the animal's head until it fell down dead. They left the carcass slightly covered with snow so the owner of the trap would be able to claim his pelt.

Kathleen's letters were piling up in Norway House with no one wanting to go for them, so Jack got an idea. He knew his beloved Tommy, a small, efficient, intelligent animal, was capable of making the trip. In early December, he hitched him up to a toboggan and set out with Bobbie Chubb as his guide.

Fortune smiled on the arduous 180-mile trip over snow and ice. On the way, a couple asked Jack to baptize their baby son Evangeline. In Norway House, the Gaudins were in bed sick so Jack preached for them. His feet were sore from trekking in a pair of ill-fitting boots, which the school principal noticed. He took pity and sold him his own pair cheaply. Then the HBC factor gave him a deal on a new toboggan. The twenty-seven pieces of mail Jack picked up included several from grateful members of his former congregations.

In a Sunday School 'budget letter' of dozens in one envelope, a girl inquired if the boys on the reserve were good-looking. A mother of three boys thanked him for having saved her marriage. All Jack wanted from life was to help somebody and be a true friend but he found it difficult to assess whether he was doing any good. When Kathleen read all this she wrote, "I think you've found the biggest secret of how to make life happy for yourself and others. It makes me look around and see if there's not somebody I can help a little more."

Saving the best for the last, Jack put the six letters Kathleen wrote in chronological order and sat on his free cot in the residential school reading and re-reading them, pretending to be living with her. She said his account of how he canoed to a prospector's camp at Knee Lake in September, and carried a detonator in one hand and 75 lbs of dynamite sticks in the other over a portage, read like a novel. Only it was better because it was real life. She could picture him eating sourdough bread around a camp-fire outside a lean-to, going with his guide to shoot a duck for supper, panning for gold and staking a claim. In that letter Jack had said he was greedy for love and wanted to have her with him all the time. No comment on that.

He loved Kathleen's scoop on the Prince of Wales' visit to receive the key to Portsmouth:

"My parents went to the Presentation of the Freedom Ceremony in the Guildhall when a rather amusing incident occurred. I think you heard, when you were here, what kind of a man our Mayor Privett is—a great lover of ceremony and etiquette and

very hopeful that this visit of the Prince will bring him a knighthood or even a baronetcy. Well, the ceremony proceeded as it should until the moment came for the Town Clerk to step forward with a book for the Prince to sign. He placed it on the table in front of him and the Mayor pulled from his pocket a beautiful silver pen with a new nib (no doubt destined to be handed down as an heirloom to future generations of Privetts as the pen with which the Prince of Wales signed when he was presented with the Freedom of the City, etc. etc. etc.) and handed it to the Prince.

"But, behold, there was no ink. The Mayor scowled, the Town Clerk hastened to ask the reporters for some—but there was none. Then Alderman Foster, who hopes to get a knighthood before the Mayor and between whom and the Mayor there is little love lost, quietly got up and handed the Prince his fountain pen. Somebody in the Town Hall will suffer because of the missing (l)ink."

Before he left for Oxford House, Jack cabled greetings to the Ward family to be delivered on Christmas Day. By the time he made it home through a snowstorm with two toboggans loaded with presents and food, he had never in all his life been so happy to see a couch and a radio. Tommy had made the first round trip by horse from Oxford House to Norway House and he had cut two days off the time it would have taken any dog team.

Kathleen got into "too great a whirl of gaiety for such a sober-minded individual," what with going to see amateur Shakespearean productions, and professional London revues trying out in Portsmouth. She transformed the Portsea girls into white angels for their Christmas concert, sang in the philharmonic society's production of Faust and played games at friends' house parties. By day, she was "glued to the café," her fingers in a perpetual state of stickiness from putting cakes out on plates. The slippers that arrived in a slipshod parcel from the Oxford House mission elated her and the cable from Canada added fizz to an otherwise flat Christmas Day. She sent Jack a copy of several Christmas magazines.

The climax was the mayor's ball on New Year's Eve. "About 1200 guests were present so you may guess what a brilliant assembly it was, what with the pretty decorations, the ladies' frocks and the bright uniforms of military and naval men. To my great surprise (this is a little bit of swank) my frock, a cherry and silver-colored one, was very much admired—one lady said she thought it was the most striking one there. I'm sure that was quite an accident; I've never set out to achieve that kind of notoriety. But I'm glad people liked it." Jack's New Year's, called *kesagow* (kissing day), was anything but brilliant. He spent it lost in a maze of lakes and bushes on the way into God's Lake with his old guide, William Grieves, who was half blind.

Being non aboriginal, Jack had to take Tommy off the reserve to haul wood. It was a lot quicker and cheaper than hiring a York boat and six men to bring in wood in the summer time. You could get as much as you wanted for $35, the cost of hiring two men to cut it. Even when the thermometer said -12 F, the cattle were still out pasturing and Jack was wearing light clothing. He wrote, "We

43

suffer little or nothing from the cold up here, although our friends down east think we must almost perish."

When the temperature settled at -49 F, he stayed inside to "read, read, read and look at seed catalogues." In mid-February the bright moon and sun alternated so the sky was never untended.

To his dismay, two of Jack's theology pals dropped out of Indian mission work after trying it for less than a year. "All mission work looks romantic and appealing at first but on the field of action it is full of drudgery and disappointment. Still, I love these northern skies, the stars, the frosty air, the cheery fire and these dark-skinned, primitive folk. They are so tantalizing and yet so much in need of a bit of intelligent, patient interest. It is neither promising nor charming but that is precisely why I want to stick with it. If I carry out a third of my dreams no one will say I have thrown my life away or buried it in the bush." A blizzard of snow did almost bury him when he went to Bear Crossing Lake in mid-March to bring 15-year-old Alfie Jowsie in for school. His parents, who were trappers, would pick him up in spring.

Soon the sun would begin to melt the four feet of snow lying like lead over Oxford Lake but now nothing stirred for a month. Alfie became so attached to Jim he stayed up looking out the window for him if he went out at night. A splendid mail arrived containing all the British Christmas magazines and a book. In all, Jack got seventy letters full of good news. These were the optimistic twenties—taxes were going down, farm values were rising, his salary was going up. . .

Slippers made for an Indian princess, and a whiff of spring, lifted Kathleen's mood

5. A Letter of Life or Death Importance

A whiff of spring in England put Kathleen in the mood to visit the unwedded mothers' home, where she was a volunteer, and to think about tennis. She had never quit crowing over last summer's victory when she and Elizabeth had beaten Jack and Walter. Kathleen asked Jack how the United Church observed Lent and how its order of service differed from the Anglican one. She took the Portsea girls to see a missionary exhibit at the Guildhall, not just once but twice, and asked Jack questions about Oxford House in winter. Her interest in these topics gave him hope.

On April 9, 1927 the last dog team of the season left Oxford House over the ice for Norway House bearing an urgent letter. By the time it arrived in Portsmouth, the year of not-giving-up-hope which a suitor had been promised would be almost expired:

"My Dear Kathleen,

"I have been trying hard to rethink the entire situation as it exists between you and me. Sometimes I think how foolish I have been to even think of you as anything but a friend, first because I'm too ordinary a fellow and second because I'm in very unattractive work. And then something happens to make me feel better. I say to myself I won't always be living away back here and my hopes are rekindled.

"Does everyone pass through such periods of discouragement and encouragement, I wonder? They come to me as regularly as the moons but somehow I always manage to come out on top so I don't worry too much about them. Sometimes I think I am a somebody and other times I'm only Farmer John with his overalls on. When I am in the former mood I sing Nobody But You Dear, Nobody But You and when in the latter mood I don't sing at all. I just saw wood.

"I hope you don't mind my pulling the curtains back and letting you have a glimpse of my inmost reflections. I feel very priggish writing to you as I have been doing all the time, wondering whether you like me or not. Tell me, won't you Kathleen, whether you like me well enough to give me a chance to win you. I will look

forward with life and death interest to your answer when the first
canoe arrives.

"With love, Jack."

The interlude of waiting for a reply drew on as Jack hauled
wood. One of the worst snow storms of the year created eight-foot
drifts on April 20th. But by June the people of Oxford House were
basking in California-like sunshine and had forgotten all that. The
first canoe, on June 16th, brought six letters from Kathleen,
obviously written before she got his crucial one. She wrote that at
the annual meeting of the sponsors of her favorite charities she had
an impulse to screw up her treasurer's report and throw it at the
audience. "So much for me and public speaking." She had been to
see The Wooing of Katherine Parr and discovered she was a very
romantic person underneath her cold exterior. ("Dear me, what am I
saying?")

Meanwhile, Tommy balked at having to haul manure for
Jack's gardens but he did it. The seeds sprouted quickly in the long
days, when the evening glow never really disappeared. It only
shifted to the north and east to become the morning glow. Jim left at
the end of school but Alfie and two trappers remained in *Mission
House*. Five prospectors arrived and two mining experts came up to
verify last year's gold find at Knee Lake. Jack put his guests to work
washing dishes, carrying water and helping prepare meals. He
insisted that anyone who stayed with him act decently and attend
church. The prospectors were not rough and uncouth, as one might
assume. They were well read, widely traveled men who jumped with

ease from Africa to Alaska in conversation. They gave Jack a concoction of citronella, camphor, carbolic acid and castor oil to repel mosquitoes.

Jack had to force himself to deal with the pile of letters from Kathleen which did not contain her answer to his heartfelt plea. He tried to sympathize with her efforts to entertain the French fleet at a ball held in their honor. When she said, "I am not a social butterfly; I really prefer the simple life," he replied, "That's what we have up here all right" and enclosed a picture of his house with the outhouse some distance away. In answer to her questions about winter, he said the people wore woolen clothes, not furs. He had a water-hole in the lake, which he kept open by using an ice chisel, and at sunset he drove Blackie and Tommy down for a drink. Then he filled two pails of water and carried them up to the house on a home-made yoke.

Just now, three men were working in his gardens and the oats, buckwheat, millet, turnips, carrots, peas, beans, parsnips, tomatoes, radishes, cauliflower and cabbage were already up. To follow were Sudan grass, potatoes, lettuce, beets, sun flowers and corn. He had planted a dozen different kinds of flowers and was waiting to see what they were.

As he was writing on June 26th, a letter was brought to the door and Jack tore it open. Then he dropped it to the floor in despair. He had to write again:

"Kathleen my dear,

"The mail has just arrived and I have before me your letter of June 2nd in which you remarked that you had not heard from me

for six weeks. If that's the case, a letter from me, a most important one, has gone astray. It left here on April 9th and should have reached you about the middle of May at the latest. It makes me sick to think we can't trust even the poor mail service we do have.

"In that letter I told you a whole lot of things about myself, among them being the longing in my heart to have your companionship through life. I think of you continuously and when at my best I feel that I can't get along without you. Sometimes I feel that, in all fairness to you, I should not ask you to share life with me. But most of the time the future seems rosy and I feel confident I could make you happy. As the days come and go I seem to want you more and more. I know you are giving me every consideration you possibly can and I know too that you will have to love me a great deal because, in the eyes of the world at least, I have not a great deal to offer you. One thing I feel proud of is that I have a group of friends who are the very finest folk in the world. As far as living up here is concerned, from the point of view of experience it is most desirable. The cold is not a factor to be feared for wood is cheap and it is not difficult to keep the house warm. The isolation is the biggest drawback but if I had only you to be my companion and helpmate I would not mind that in the least.

"But, while I tell you all this, I know that the outward aspects of our life together would neither attract nor detract you i.e. in any deciding way. It is because I love you on account of your mind and character—but also, I must admit, because of your charming appearance—that I would dare to ask you to be my wife. Your letter

received today is a real disappointment but the delay will be
forgotten a hundred times if your answer now is favorable.

"With love, Jack."

The next day an unexpected canoe paddled in and this time
there was no mistaking the pretty, lavender paper postmarked
Portsmouth. The letter containing Jack's earnest plea for Kathleen's
love had dallied transatlantically for eight weeks but, when it finally
arrived, she had acted swiftly to relieve his agony:

"My Dear Jack,

"I am very glad you have asked, Jack, because ever since
you left here last year I have been in a very unsettled frame of mind
and cannot even now say where I stand. However, I feel I owe it to
you to tell you, as far as possible, some of the moods and thoughts to
which I have been subject. I leave it to you to draw your own
conclusions and act accordingly. First of all, I am quite certain that
when I said "No" last June I was doing the right thing. However
much my mind may have urged me to say "Yes," deep down I had a
feeling I simply could not. You were not prepared to accept that
answer as final and I felt, as you wanted me so badly, I could do
nothing else but go back and think the whole matter out again.

"At times I was, and still am, seized by attacks of pure funk. I
think how very little I know you and have seen you, and imagine all
the terrible things that might happen if we married and were not
happy. And then I think what a fool I am, and realize that I am not of
a nature to be violently or passionately in love. For me a marriage
based on deep, trusting friendship would be ideal and the only one

possible. And I do believe, Jack, that you and I have similar tastes and would get along well together.

"I have prayed a lot and refuse to lose my faith that whatever we decide will be for the best. And that brings me to what I believe will be the best course of action. If you really think it worth your while I would like you to come over again when you can be spared for a few weeks from your work. I think there is a sporting chance that I may throw in my lot with yours. You have never been long out of my thoughts during the last year and many times I have badly wanted to see you.

"On the other hand, Jack, I want you to face the fact that I may know quite definitely and finally that I do not want to marry you. There are times when I feel that the last thing I want to do is to marry you, or for that matter, any man. But I think if we could meet again we could quite definitely find where we stand and decide our future relations. I am very ashamed I do not know my own mind better and have not liked writing this letter. Put so badly, one's thoughts take on an unpleasant and distasteful aspect. But I think you will understand and I want you to know what I feel and think. Now, I am perfectly aware that you may dislike me, upon discovering the state of my mind, and think me a most objectionable little prig. Or, you may not be prepared to make another trip to England. But if you still do want me very badly, Jack, and think it worth your while, I shall be very pleased to see you.

"In any case, I want you to do just what you like—don't hurry to decide, but really think what will be the best. I shall

understand and not be hurt because, above everything, I want to make you happy. Do not, by the way, worry about your work. I am quite prepared to share it with you wherever it may be. And if I do decide to marry you I will not keep you waiting long.

"Kathleen."

Jack did not hesitate to reply:

"My Dear Kathleen:

"I do appreciate the spirit of frankness you show in your letter and think I can, to some extent at least, understand your feelings. We have not seen much of each other, it is true, and yet I seem to know what you are doing all the time. You can't say that of me because I don't write such good letters as you do. But I think I will be able to go over and see you in October. I have been counting on going as far as Winnipeg at that time and can arrange to go on, coming back here about December 15th so as to help the teacher prepare for the Christmas entertainment. While my feelings will be those of a gambler making his last throw, I am greatly encouraged when you say there is a sporting chance you may cast your lot with mine.

"I too have prayed about this matter a great deal and must confess I have been selfish and at times rather insistent—like the importunate widow. I know it is possible to imagine all sorts of calamities that might befall us but doesn't every young couple face the same possibility? And why should we look for the ill rather than the good? None of the evil things I have feared the most have ever

happened and I strongly doubt they will provided my attitude to life is the correct one.

"I am so glad you added those remarks about my work. If there is one thing that is dearer to me than anything else in the world it is my profession and, perhaps I should add, my citizenship. I am proud to be a Christian minister and proud to be a Canadian citizen. No other work appeals to me like this work yet I am fully aware it has no monopoly on Christian service. You are just great to say what you do about being ready to share my work in such a whole-hearted manner—if the major question is once settled. Well, we will talk about all that if I can possibly manage to go over in October. In the meantime we will be just the same real friends that we have been all along.

"With love, Jack"

Cree women and girls liked Kathleen's picture and wondered who she was

6. Gambling on a Sporting Chance

Charles Lindbergh was guest of honor on Parliament Hill in Ottawa for Canada's 60th birthday, while Jack shared his first radishes with his men and gave them the day off from fence-building. He looked forward to the time when these wards of the Government of Canada would be full citizens of the country. On Jubilee Sunday, a day of national thanksgiving, the whole nation tuned into a simultaneous broadcast with the order of service written by federal MPs. To Jack this was a historic step towards the Dominion of Canada becoming a Christian commonwealth.

He told the Cree 'Canada' was an aboriginal word and 'Dominion' was taken from the Bible. The Jews had a vision of what

54

God expected of them and, in the same way, Canadians were chosen to show how a nation may be built in peace, righteousness and sincerity, and how people of varying religions and races may live together in one nation with tolerance and honor. His dinner guest was Isaac Fletcher, the guide who had led the Duke of Connaught from Norway House to York Factory years ago.

After singing The Fairy Laundry at a rainy garden party to raise money for the unwed mothers, Kathleen wrote Jack an especially nice letter on his 30th birthday:

"My Dear Jack,

"I am most awfully glad that you think you will be able to come over in October and I hope with all my heart that I shall be able to give you an answer that will make you happy. But you understand, don't you—there is a factor in my make-up that I am not sure of and that made me feel as I did last year. I am hoping that when we meet again all my doubts and fears will disappear. Nothing would make Mummy and Daddy and the rest of the family happier than for you to be added to it—they have told me so.

"One other thing I want to say to you. You make me feel very humble when you pay such attributes to my mind and character as you did in your last two letters. I am not anywhere nearly like the wonderful person you imagine—please do modify your ideas a little or you are going to be very disappointed when we meet. I am very, very ordinary and not the least worthy of you. There, I have unburdened my mind and so will close, knowing that at any rate for

the immediate future we are still the good friends we have always been.

"Yours affectionately, Kathleen."

When Jack got this letter he went out for a walk in the starlight. Imagine that the Wards would welcome him into their family! He had feared that they mightn't, since Enid had moved so far away—but the world was getting smaller. He felt sorry for having put Kathleen in such a difficult position. Permeating his thoughts of her was a deep feeling of mystery and wonder. He visualized the two of them together, "High, high up in the sky, watching the world go by." The only direction in which he could revise his estimate of her was upwards. But he mustn't anticipate too much. At any rate they would be the best of friends. After coming home from trying to settle a quarrel between a husband, wife and mother-in-law, he pressed some garden flowers and enclosed them in a letter to Portsmouth.

Kathleen's cousin, 19-year-old Jack Bernard Ward, was bent on joining the police force in India but the family persuaded him to go to Canada, where agricultural help was needed. After an exchange of letters, Bernard was invited to work on the Kell farms at Cookstown. He excelled at horse-riding, marksmanship and swimming.

Jack said his mother, Mary Jane, would be a kind, intelligent friend but she was Irish and expected people to step around. His sister, Mabel, would do all she could to make things comfortable. His brothers, Clifton and Wilson, worked so fast no one could possibly keep up with them. Things were done in a more haphazard way than on an English farm but the output was greater. The young people were jovial because they were constantly being told this was their country and they could make it into whatever they wanted it to be. Jack was sure Bernard was "the right sort" and, from his first letters home after arriving, this appeared to be true. He said the family was wonderful, he was enjoying himself and the farm was one of the finest in Canada.

Kathleen's café did brisk business when Princess Mary passed along the street three times within one hour. Jack sent a diary letter starting with a wedding write-up:

"Monday: I was putting rolls of wire on the fence around 4:15 p.m. when young Edwin came up and said "They're ready." "Who's ready?" I asked. "The wedding" he replied. Sure enough, a hundred or more people were streaming down the road towards the church. Well, I thought to myself, if they can't give me more warning than that they will just have to wait. "You tell them I'll be ready at six o'clock," I said. Edwin went away but then the Chief came and said he had sent a boy to tell me but he must have forgotten. I took this as a bona fide excuse and went in to get changed. Usually I wear a white bow tie and wing collar but the shirt with the tie buttons was dirty so I wore a wedding-gray tie. The bride wore a white dress made out of muslin purchased at the Hudson Bay store three hours before. We got through the ceremony with Edwin translating. I took pictures on the church step and all was over by 6 p.m.

"*Tuesday: The verandah was particularly breezy and inviting so I put up an awning to shelter the hammock from the sun and read Clark Wissler's The American Indian. After supper a canoe-load of medical supplies arrived from Winnipeg and I repacked and sent on those destined for God's Lake. Then I baptized a baby at his home.*

"*Wednesday: I began to unpack and stow away 1,000 pounds of medicines, including 18 gallons of cod liver oil. The freight I ordered didn't arrive because I had forgotten to sign my check. A little three-year-old girl is suffering from some kind of brain or nervous trouble so I mixed a bottleful of sodium bromide and took it over to her. Then I called on a 14-year-old girl who is suffering from TB and gave her a bottle of cod liver oil. I always let the people try their own remedies first and only give them white man's medicine if they ask for it. Two little boys are suffering from the severest form of TB which has symptoms similar to spinal meningitis and I had to tell their parents I can do nothing for them. Many of the people have bigger families than they can care for and TB captures the weak, sickly ones.*

"*Thursday: I gave the Chief paint for the inside of the school and walked over to see how the men were doing. They didn't know they should take the pictures and blackboard off the wall so I did, and I explained that they shouldn't paint the windows. After the evening prayer meeting, I settled into my hammock to read a book on law until it got dark at 10 p.m. A canoe with an engine arrived with mail from Norway House after only two and one-half days!*

"*Wednesday: Dr. Grant, Professor of Anatomy at the University of Manitoba, is here with two men and a box of instruments. He is measuring these people—their height, stretch, cranium, mouth, nose etc.—what for, I do not know. On Sunday he spoke in church and said the doctors are hoping to be able to use these measurements to forecast which diseases an individual is most likely to contract. He is an Old Country man of the "oh-rather" type, but not a bad sort.*

"*Saturday: Mr. Barner, the superintendent of Indian missions, arrived before Dr. Grant's canoe was out of sight. He is the most delightful of superintendents, never criticizing but always inspiring. I told him about you and he was glad to hear of my plans. He doesn't think I'm gadding about too much and will try to help me get a special-rate train ticket.*

"*Monday: At a meeting yesterday the men were given a chance to ask questions or make suggestions and one man told Mr. Barner how much they like me. Such an expression of appreciation is apparently rare. He is now putting on my bathing suit for a run into the lake before we go visiting. Tomorrow there will be three services and an ordination of two elders. I asked Mr. Barner about getting a furnace and he was quite in favor so I will get that work done next summer. A few of the men are watching him very carefully as he splashes around in the lake. These people do not take advantage of their beautiful, clean lakes and rivers for bathing purposes because they suspect that going into the water makes them weak. One old man joked me that he takes two baths a year: one when he tips his canoe and the other when he falls through the ice."*

In August, Jack had more anecdotes to tell about his work:

"The airplane with the treaty party did not arrive so for four days we scanned the clouds and strained our ears. Then, in the middle of the church service, I noticed an unusual amount of whispering in the congregation, "chemanuk, chemanuk," and found that two canoes had come in. One had a flag flying."

"I invited four Americans passing through on their way to York Factory for tea. They were impressed with our people and my garden and say I have better potatoes than in Cincinnati. They asked Dulas many questions, which he answered patiently, about the Indians, their language and his wife. Alice served tea and they couldn't believe she is pure Cree, at least as pure as any people can be after six generations of association with white people. Some men who were cutting hay have returned to say they have put up five tons. It's a pleasure to find men who can be trusted to do such work. Next we'll build a stable.

"For ten years this school has been conducted with a home-made table and benches and this afternoon I nailed four boards on top of boxes. Some table! I have spoken to the Indian agent and he has promised to do his best to supply proper seats and desks."

"My associations with these people are extremely happy, except that they do have a faculty for tiring one and doing disappointing things. When one wants to speed up the rate of progress one feels the burden heavily. But if one doesn't feel that

way at times the consequence is laziness and apathy—a state of affairs I dread."

Jack was glad when Kathleen confided in him. The week of the August Bank Holiday her family deserted her to go on vacation, leaving her feeling lonely and rotten. On top of coping with an extra crowd of customers, she had to fire her kitchen maid at the café. Her work had been unsatisfactory for some time, but the last straw was when she refused to wipe the brass rods that kept the stair carpeting in place.

After Kathleen's family got back, she went to Winchester with her aunt and uncle and a friend of theirs to tour the church and hospital of St.Cross (which had a new gate.) They drove off with her uncle at the wheel and Kathleen beside him and were going along nicely when a car veered out to pass a truck and came straight at them. Kathleen was sure she was going to die! At the last split-second the hysterical driver squeezed in between them and the truck and got back on her own side of the road. The truck driver cursed, Uncle turned apoplectic, and Auntie and her friend screamed. Kathleen, however, did not experience the least fear or thrill. Her famously lousy nerves were shockproof in a real emergency!

Amid an abundance of sweet peas, phlox, cosmos, marigolds, poppies and pansies, Jack basked in the perfect days and balmy nights of early September. Then he stopped dreaming and got started on an important project—a new winter trail. He wanted to link Oxford House up with the new HBC rail line at Mile 214 or Pikwitonei (meaning sore mouth) 140 miles distant. If he succeeded, another group of traders would be able to come in. When he first came north, he thought the HBC was a benefactor to the people. But now he saw it as getting a poor, ignorant aboriginal into a corner, extracting his fur for the lowest market price and charging him the sky for his food.

Jack had discussed the matter of the trail with the district manager of the HBC and, when he saw how emphatically opposed he was, he decided he absolutely must go ahead. The trail would be mostly over lake ice with only about twenty miles of bush to be cut through. He would hire Cree who knew the territory to do the work in sections. Even if it cost him $200, it would be worthwhile. The first day Jack and two men working for the whole day were able to cut through only about one mile of bush. It was very slow going but the men would continue working while he was away.

A tennis partner arrived just in time to help Jack practice his game, which was atrocious except for the odd, spectacular ace. Nelson Gaudin, the Norway House missionaries' son, was replacing Jim as schoolteacher and roommate. Nelson was more fluent than Jack in Cree, so more people dropped into *Mission House* to talk verbosely.

Jack wanted to take off in mid-September and be in Toronto to attend centenary celebrations at the university but someone broke into Dulas' store. The RCMP arrived, a rowdy council meeting was held and Jack waited for the hullabaloo to settle down. He was walking a cow on a leash when she bolted, dragging him and whipping off his glasses so they were lost in the bush. He couldn't read without his eyes getting sore. Then a vicious head-wind came up, locking in his canoe.

While Jack waited to get going, he dreamt up an amusing sermon. He pretended otherwise but it was really just for himself and Kathleen. This was 'their' sermon. The text, "Put out thy hand and take it by the tail" [Exodus 4:4], depicts the Lord placing a serpent before Moses and telling him to pick it up. The points it illustrates are (1) Do not be afraid to attempt the hard task (2) There is a safe way to begin, and (3) The Lord will never ask anyone to do anything which is not feasible. When Moses reached down and picked up the serpent, it became a rod, a symbol that the hardest task by an almost magical process becomes our main source of support. "I don't, of course, accept this story as actual history but it sparkles with interest all the same," Jack wrote. Finally he shoved off on September 28th, leaving Isaac and Nelson in charge of the mission.

A wedding and honeymoon flight across the Channel were organized hastily

7. A Fairy Tale Marriage Gets Off to a Rickety Start

When Jack got to Winnipeg, he bought a train ticket to Toronto and was glad to have sixty-seven cents left in his pocket. After the overnight trip, he went straight to Burwash Hall, the men's residence at Victoria College, and had a bath, shave and breakfast. He withdrew $100 from his bank account on Yonge St., had his hair cut and bought a suit, shoes, shirt, gloves and hat. Then he visited the dentist, who extracted nine rotted teeth and fitted him for a temporary plate to be picked up the next day. That done, Jack bought a new pair of glasses at the optician's and hopped on a bus for a quick trip to Cookstown to visit his family and share his news. His comings and goings made an interesting gossip item for the social columnist of the local paper and Wilson paid him $500 for past work on the farm. Back in Toronto, Jack bought a boat ticket to England and boarded the overnight train for Ottawa. He had breakfast with his sister, Clara (who was in town for a conference) in the new Chateau Laurier hotel, then bought a passport and continued on to Montreal.

Jack embarked on the *Ascania* on October 14th, clutching a fox fur he had bought for $50 at the railway station. Ernie Taylor, his Navy buddy who was now with the Montreal YMCA, his wife Mary and their two children waved him on. From Quebec City, Jack sent a cable to Portsmouth to give the Wards his time of arrival ten days hence. Then 'Cinder Jack' settled down in a deck chair as his fairy godmother smiled down on the bumpkin transformed into Prince Charming.

When Kathleen looked into Jack's eyes at Cosham railway station in Southampton, all her fears and doubts fell away. She was positive everything was going to be all right. However, to make sure her misgivings were gone for good, she decided to watch over her emotions for three days and four nights to see if any bad feelings returned. On October 27th, as they waited to catch a bus to London to have lunch with friends, she told him she was going to marry him. They picked out a diamond ring at a jewelry shop in Trafalgar Square and that night there was great rejoicing in *The Cottage*.

Elizabeth had little time to plan a wedding, since Jack had to sail away on November 5th, but she phoned as many relatives and close friends as possible. Everyone pitched in. The maid cleaned Jack's clerical collar with a bread crust since they couldn't find a supplier of new ones. The bishop in charge of the local Anglican parish of St. George granted a quick marriage license after Kathleen signed an affidavit swearing that she resided in Waterlooville. The night before the wedding, Walter drew Jack aside and warned him honorably, "She has a terrible temper."

They said their vows on the rainy morning of Nov. 2, 1927, plighting their troth and promising "to love and honor thee only, forsaking all others, till death us do part." The only picture of the bride in a navy blue suit wearing a hat and fox fur is blurry. They left their guests to linger at *The Cottage* over coffee and cake while they caught the noon luncheon train to London. That night they slept in the honeymoon suite of the Hotel Belgravia.

Early next morning, Kathleen and Jack soared off on their married adventures in Imperial Airway's 12-passenger deluxe Silver Wing flying out of Croydon airport. It was a four-hour leap over the English Channel. Kathleen's aunt, uncle and three cousins watched them taxi down the grass; there was no runway. The canvas of the airplane was so thin that her uncle remarked he could have poked his finger through it.

In Paris, the bride and groom took a Cook's tour, window-shopped, lunched at Webers and stayed at the Hotel Greffulhe. They didn't sleep; love clamored after every precious moment they had together. In the morning, their flight from Le Bourget airport was delayed for one-and-one-half hours due to fog. Up in the air, it was too noisy to talk but Kathleen enjoyed her box lunch while Jack, sitting across the aisle, groaned with airsickness. She always was a good sailor. When they landed in London, a stewardess rushed up and said, "Are you all right? You've had a bumpy ride, haven't you?" They felt like pioneers in the air, although it was seventeen years since Louis Berliot first flew over the Channel.

That night, Elizabeth and Walter hosted a wedding banquet for twenty-six people in Kimbells' Hotel with a menu of consommé julienne, fillet of sole cardinal, lamb cutlets jardinière, roast chicken with chips and cress, maraschino cream ice, Charlotte vanilla, fruit salad, dessert and coffee. Jack didn't want to take Kathleen into Oxford House in winter so she would stay in England to prepare her trousseau, say her farewells and then join him in June.

The next day, Jack stood transfixed on the deck of the *Alaunia* as his beautiful bride smiled at him roguishly from shore, waving a white silk scarf and blowing kisses. He couldn't feel sad even in parting. Surely the time would pass quickly with so much to do and anticipate. "I hope and pray we will bear up under the strain of lonesomeness," he wrote. "We have tasted the sweetness of married life and a wonderful experience lies ahead. We must philosophize and rationalize our fate and then things don't seem so bad." Each night they gave each other a big, imaginary hug.

Jack had a risky trip ahead of him. He was planning to take a team of horses through the unbroken trail between the HBC rail line and Oxford House. This had never been done before but he told himself he was neither going to freeze nor starve to death. On arrival in Canada he went to Cookstown to tell his family he was married. Wilson told him not to worry about his trip; he always got through.

Passionate love letters from Kathleen now crossed the Atlantic Ocean. Jack replied, "Hitherto I have been snatching such nourishment as I might from the crumbs you dropped but now you have placed before me a sumptuous feast. It is such a wonderful feeling to know there's one genuine girl who really loves you. Some people might think that what we have done is risky but we're not worried about that, are we? True marriage is a project for artists, not scientists."

Jack inquired at the Manitoba parliament buildings in Winnipeg as to whether anyone in The Pas sold horses. While waiting for the answer, he stocked up on supplies and sent Kathleen a money order to buy herself a Paris frock, since she hadn't had time to find one on their honeymoon. He wanted to tell their news to his old flame, Esther Gaudin, who was teaching here, but how could he without disrupting the marital pattern? He solved the dilemma by telling Kathleen 'his lordship' was asking 'her ladyship's' permission and she was instantly granting it. Esther invited him to her landlady's for tea and he took her out to the Chocolate Shoppe. Jack reported to Kathleen that he had lunched with "a beautiful, charming, attractive, congenial and intelligent young lady but not nearly as beautiful, charming, attractive, congenial and intelligent as my wife."

The answer from The Pas was "No." Since it cost too much to freight a team of horses up the line, Jack just bought one, Big Lad, who had a cheerful personality. At 3 a.m. they boarded a mixed freight train and for four days swayed and ricocheted up the west side of Lake Winnipeg. They traveled at night and had to shunt when the passenger train usurped the track. At a stopover in Swan River, Jack knocked on the door of the parsonage and was just in time to address an area-wide girls' conference, talk to the Sunday School, assist at church and help entertain the Anglican minister and the local member of parliament over tea. Next day, the train passengers walked a quarter of a mile to a lumber camp for noon dinner.

Up beyond The Pas, Father and Big Lad, with their new toboggan and 800 pounds of supplies, were dumped out into a snow bank at Mile 137 (Wabowden.) It was midnight and -30 F, but an acquaintance-of-an-acquaintance from Beeton, Ontario lived here and sheltered Jack. Early next morning, he made a deal with a man who was returning from jail to guide him to Cross Lake in return for pulling his possessions. Big Lad didn't want to have anything to do with that miserable-looking big worm (the toboggan.) The load kept upsetting on the crooked trail and they had to repack several times before they got going. It was hard, even with the wind in their backs, but they managed to jog into a camp at about 6 p.m. Just as the sun was setting, the moon rose in the sky and laughed at Jack. "Never mind," it seemed to say, "I'm here."

They set out before sunrise and watched patches of forest light up here and there in a magical panorama of white, green and gold. As the trail wound around a long, strung-out lake they expected at any moment to turn a corner and see the sun. Finally, Old Sol made his entrance in full glory. There was not a cloud in the sky. Not a sight except forest and snow. Not a sound but the slide of a toboggan and the crunch of a footstep and hoof. "Whatever else I'm coming home to," Jack thought, "I'm returning to beautiful nature."

At Cross Lake, a letter from Kathleen was waiting for him. He sat out a three-day storm at the home of the missionaries before tackling the 130-mile trek on to Oxford House. The route ahead was seldom trod by man and never before by horse. Big Lad would have to follow, rather than pull, so Jack hired two men with a team of dogs to break the trail.

For four days, they scrambled through the roughest of all bush, often on hand and knee, while Big Lad picked his way behind them like a perfect gentleman. Jack had never had such cold hands or sore feet. It was terribly inconvenient trying to eat and sleep outside at -30 F. If you put up your hand to shield your face from the fire, the back of it burned while the palm froze. You could not sit or lie down because you had to keep rotating. The most irritating thing was having to listen to his guides snore while he tossed and turned under his eiderdown, longing for a comfortable bed. The difference must be due to generations of conditioning. They curled up in little balls under their thin gray blankets, the way their dogs did under a layer of snow, and let their breath keep them warm.

Elizabeth Barrett Browning's lines, "Earth's crammed with heaven and every common bush afire with God", came to Jack's mind. He could sort of layer the aboriginal beliefs onto his own, as metaphors and similes. At night the northern lights danced like the spirits of the happy hunting grounds, darting about in shoots and waves, displaying the gentle color-tints of the rainbow. At a trapper's shack on the Carrot River, Jack paid off the guides and sent them back to Cross Lake bearing a letter to Kathleen which he wrote by candlelight while sitting outdoors on a box. He loved incongruity.

The shack's owner Absalom Ougemou agreed to serve as guide for the rest of the journey. Jack pushed Big Lad along because he knew he would sleep in his own stable that night. (Horses don't sleep when they are out on the trail.) Nelson, now twenty-five pounds heavier, and the Oxford House schoolchildren spied the horse and toboggan party coming into view and ran up the lake to greet them. The trip from Thompson to Oxford House which now takes nine hours by car had taken seven days.

Jack shared his happy news with his friends and gave out the little pieces of wedding cake he had carried all the way in his pocket as a reality check. Before he fell asleep, he wrote to Kathleen to tell her he was safely home and thanked God he had a house, a roaring fire and a loving wife. The events of the past two months seemed like an improbable dream.

As Kathleen waved good-bye, a wedding gift of china was delivered to her ship

8. Kathleen Readies Herself for an Oceanic Leap

Reactions to the wedding announcements poured in, assuring Kathleen of a warm welcome in Canada in the spring. Belated references told her Jack was a wonderful person.

When Jack's college friend, Ira Perkins, got the news he almost went berserk:

"You've sent my house into a riot! You went down to a count of nine like [world heavyweight boxing champion] Tunney. A dash from the North Pole by dog team, tin-canning across the Atlantic, a

73

ring on the finger of the Queen of England, planting a kiss on her lips, taking her for an airplane trip, good-bye dearie, a dash back, fresh dog team and back at the North Pole before the fire went out. To think that I roomed for a year with a fellow like that!"

Jack's Navy buddy, Ezra Parkhouse, who had also been invited to the Wards' home for tea and had been following the tennis courtship since it began, sent just two words, "Who won?"

After all the excitement of getting married, Kathleen spent a miserable day at home alone with her mother. Jack had arrived on October 25th, wed her on November 2nd and left her on November 5th. She had married a man she had been with for only two weeks out of her whole life. She had agreed to be the lifelong work partner of a minister whom she had never heard preach. She was abandoning her family, her friends and her country. How could such a sensible person as herself have done such a thing?

'Mrs. Knell,' as she was introduced at a singing engagement, gave up drinking alcohol and smoking cigarettes in order to set a good example in her new role as a minister's wife. She had a lot of questions to ask of her husband, such as What color are your eyes? Should I bring my hockey stick? What about my silver chest? He told her she could bring anything she wanted, since the canoe was as commodious a method of travel as the train, but not her golf clubs— and her hockey stick only if she was very attached to it. She should pack warm underwear in her 'wanted' trunk, since the ocean crossing might be chilly. In reply to what rallying cry she could take up in place of Rule Britannia, he suggested Vive la Compagnie.

74

Jack whet Kathleen's appetite for Canada by raving about two northern delicacies the people shared with him, moose nose and baked sturgeon. He had had the new toboggan converted into a cariole, the most comfortable conveyance imaginable. Blackie had given birth to a calf, Cinderella, and was providing cream for coffee and a supply of milk for the people. An earlier effort to bring in cows had failed when the Indian agent had said, "You will have to feed them sufficient hay." This was interpreted as, "some fish and hay." The people didn't have enough fish for themselves and their dogs, let alone cows.

As a faithful knight in the service of the church, Jack was battling frustrations and setbacks. Success depended on co-operation between Church and Government and on setting an example. Yet not one white man came to the New Year service. Indian agent Gordon came up for the trial of a man for last fall's break-in and agreed to speak in church but overslept and let the people down. Jack's blood boiled when a man who was sent to bring mail and goods up from Norway House came back empty-handed, due to a petty dispute at the HBC post.

The supply of animals, especially beaver and muskrat, dwindled. Traditional ways couldn't compete with white trappers' methods of hunting an area out and moving on. Some aboriginal hunters traveled over an area of 300 square miles to feed their families. George White, a prospector and trapper who lived in a cabin at Knee Lake, was threatening and cursing and not letting them get at their traps. The next time George came to stay at *Mission*

House, Jack told him he didn't want to be seen as harboring someone unfriendly to the people. George had to sleep at the HBC post instead.

For two years, Jack had been imbuing Kathleen with the right attitudes to get along in Canada and now wrote, "You will have hosts of new friends, rich experiences in service and adventure and a home built on the foundation stones of love, sympathy and patience. Just because you are giving up so much, I am going to try doubly hard to make things pleasant and nice for you. You have all the qualities that spell success and need not feel a single tremor."

Kathleen was making an impression on both sides of the ocean. At Oxford House, Mr. Gordon looked at her picture and said, "She has strong eyes." The Cree mothers asked who she was and Jack answered, *"okimow squao"* (queen.) They said "eh" knowingly and asked exactly how big she was. She was also the toast of Portsmouth, juggling appointments and engagements. Most difficult of all to part with were the Portsea girls, who had become her friends. Three of them came to the café for help with their lines for the Christmas concert. Two of them expected to become domestic servants but the third, a hawker's daughter, wrote stories and wanted to go on stage. At the annual bazaar at Wesley Chapel the four Misses Greene, who ran a private school Kathleen attended when very small, said they had always known she'd be a missionary.

George White had stopped bothering the Cree and the unaccustomed quiet made them even more uneasy. They alerted Jack who, with a sense of foreboding, trekked with the HBC factor and a guide out to George's cabin, fearing the worst. They found his frozen body lying on the floor with his rifle beside it. They sent for the RCMP who came up to investigate and determined that he had killed himself. Jack helped bring the corpse in, thawed it out on his dining room table and fixed it up for a funeral. This tragedy was a big blow to the small community of white men around the reserve who stayed in each other's homes, argued vociferously, cut each other's hair and shared three bathing suits. Last year, George had given a talk in church on how to make sourdough bread. This year, his hopes were dashed when the gold claims he staked proved worthless.

In April, the families came in from winter camp dragging their dead family members behind them. Jack figured he could cut thirty days off his and Kathleen's separation by going out over the ice, rather than waiting for the thaw. The Portsmouth people would think Canada an inhospitable place if spring didn't come until June. He asked Kathleen if she could set sail in early May and sent her the money to reserve cabin-class passage.

On April 16th, Jack set out with a guide on the trail he had been hacking to the railway line, hoping to visit Cree encampments along the way. Instead, they got lost for a whole day, until they found a fishing camp at 2 a.m. After resting up, Jack felt so good he walked ahead of the dogs all the way to Pikwitonei. The minister's wife pressed his trousers and he helped her husband with the Sunday service.

In Winnipeg, a marconigram from Kathleen said she would arrive on the *Ausonia* on May 14th. Jack had expected her to be on the *Metagami* on May 4th, so now he had time to go see his mother. But in Toronto, on May 2nd, he got word from his sister, Clara, that an unsigned telegram had arrived in Cookstown saying, "Come quickly. *Metagami* docks May 4th." Jack was mystified but decided he'd better hurry on to Montreal. When he got there Ernie Taylor told him he, not Kathleen, had sent the telegram. Meanwhile, Mary Jane's temper flared. Not only was her daughter-in-law English (as if a Canadian girl wasn't good enough), but she sent unsigned telegrams which upset people's plans. Jack cooled his heels for ten days in Montreal, painting a baby carriage and speaking to YMCA youth.

Clutching a bouquet of lilies of the valley, Kathleen waved good-bye to her family and England. Just before her boat pulled out, a friend from the café had a wedding present delivered —a 30-piece tea set of fine black and white china decorated with silhouettes of fairies. The steward said it could not land in Canada; the straw it was packed in might carry foot and mouth disease. So, Kathleen repacked it in the warm underwear in her trunk.

Having found out from the ship's recreation director that the *Ausonia* was carrying Polish and Czech emigrants in steerage, Kathleen was curious to see what they looked like. She wrote in her journal, "They are extraordinary folk who lie about the deck in weird positions, some of them on top of each other. The smell of garlic around their cabins is appalling." They packed it in with their clothes to ward off disease. The former captain of the *Lusitania* was at the helm of the ship and invited Kathleen to sit at his table.

The sea was calm, with steady rain and misty patches, as the ship entered the St. Lawrence River and Kathleen saw the contours of a rugged, barren-looking land studded with tall pine and fir trees huddling together. Gray rocks interrupted brown grass and vegetation. Little villages nestled near the shore, each distinguished by its tiny church and spire. White houses with bright, green roofs stood out against a dark background. At Father Point, a pinnace arrived bearing a Canadian pilot and the mail, including letters from Jack and Walter for Kathleen.

Jack saw the *Ausonia* come into view and had no trouble spotting what looked like the last war bride from WWI. She was wearing a fur coat and beehive hat purchased especially for Canada. On one arm she was bearing the dozen red roses he had cabled to her in Quebec City and, in the other, she was cradling a newspaper package. That was his girl—so refined and yet so realistic! The package contained the dress she wore at the ship's farewell party and had left hanging in her cabin cupboard, where the steward noticed it. At Customs, she had to separate what she needed from what could be sent on so she retrieved her underwear from her china in public on the station platform. She called this her first housekeeping problem in Canada.

Jack immediately delivered on his promise to provide her with new experiences: lunch with the Taylors in Montreal and a bear hug from Ezra in Kingston. They dined at Clara's and close friends' homes in Toronto, plus seeing the university, the Normal School (where Clara was studying), Eaton's and the Board of Missions. At the home of Superintendent Barner, Kathleen had her first taste of creamed corn.

The next day, Jack's brother Clifton came down from Cookstown in his car and drove them the thirty miles back home. Kathleen was fascinated to see farms separated by fences, not hedges, and wood-frame houses with big chimneys—a sign of the central heating she had heard about. After driving up a beautiful maple lane to a comfortable house, they got a raucous welcome from the dog and the parrot Jack had brought back from Mexico. She met the rest of Jack's family: mother Mary Jane, sister Mabel, brother Wilson, his wife Maggie and children Mary and Albert.

Kathleen hardly recognized her cousin Bernard in overalls, digging a hole for a new pump underneath the windmill. Jack put on his old hat, cautioned her to stay out of the mud and showed her around, leaving the women to prepare a hearty meal. After dinner, Kathleen was given wedding presents: a broad-bladed serving knife and other sterling silver pieces, lace and damask table linens, Pyrex cookware and a tortoise-shell dresser set. Mabel gave her a comforter stuffed with wool from her pet lamb, and the money for six hens.

Although Jack had said Mary Jane would be a kind and intelligent friend, she had not written to welcome Kathleen into the family, as had Clara and Mabel. In an effort to get into her good graces, Kathleen said she was 'green' and didn't even know how to iron a man's shirt. Mary Jane heated up an iron on the wood stove, fitted it with a handle, put up the ironing board, got a shirt, and sat down with the other women to be entertained. It was a great release for them to laugh at Kathleen's struggle but she was mortified.

Mary Jane could not understand why the Wards had sent Bernard to them. He had no interest in nor aptitude for farm work. His real name was Jack and that's what she called him. He seemed to imagine the family's two 100-acre farms (one belonging to her and one to Wilson) to be far grander than they were. Of course none of Mary Jane's underlying grumbling erupted, and Jack didn't go looking for trouble. If he had any suspicions, he just sloughed them off. Kathleen drew Jack into another room for a whispered conversation behind the closed door but he assured her they liked her. Then she sat alone in a corner of the front room and read a book.

Jack drove Kathleen over to visit other relatives' homes on luxuriant hundreds of acres of rolling, verdant land. She was most impressed with the beautiful cellars where potatoes, vegetables and fuel were stored. The meals were informal, compared to those in England, but were served on fine-quality china and table linens and always included cake. "The Canadian woman runs a home, raises children and yet finds time to study and even take university courses," Kathleen wrote home. "There is no place like this for making you realize you are essentially a man or a woman with a mind and body to be used in good, healthy exercise." She sat on a horse, watched a windmill go up, posed for a picture with the sheared lamb and was welcomed from the pulpit of Cookstown United Church.

Fortunately, Kathleen could not see what lay ahead. Weeks later, Bernard had a nervous breakdown. He became very religious and the family feared he would do himself harm. They got him to hospital, with the help of the police constable and a neighbor, and contacted his parents. He was put on a boat for England as soon as he was well enough to travel. He got better but, a few years later, stepped in front of a car and was killed.

They sailed, shot small rapids, stopped at Sea Falls Portage and used stepping-stones

9. Canoeing up the Old Fur Trade Route

After leaving the farm, Kathleen and Jack hopped off the Toronto-bound bus at Richmond Hill so he could show her his boarding-house on his old preaching charge. The guests of honor were an hour late for the surprise party because they hadn't set their watches ahead to Daylight Saving Time. Everyone burst out singing Blest Be the Tie That Binds as they arrived and well-wishers kept dropping in until 10:30 p.m. The next day at Wymilwood, the girls' residence at Victoria College, the newlyweds hosted a reception for forty of Jack's friends before boarding *The National* for Winnipeg.

The scenery changed from green farmland to pines, firs, rock, brown grass, streams, lakes and swamps. Huts, a lumber camp, floating logs and isolated railway stations flashed by. At Hornepayne they stayed with the Levi Atkinsons, who used to be missionaries at Oxford House. To Kathleen, this railway town of 1200 looked like a scene from the movies. Men were sitting on the steps outside wooden shops. Little children competing in a sports day to celebrate Queen Victoria's birthday (the 24th of May) were wearing long trousers à la Jackie Coogan or wide-brimmed straw hats à la Broncho Bill. Kathleen was 300 miles away from the nearest highway and surrounded by bush yet didn't feel at all isolated as she chatted with Mrs. Atkinson about what winter clothes to buy.

In Winnipeg, Kathleen plunged into *vive-la-compagnie* life at the annual conference of the Lake Winnipeg Presbytery of the Manitoba Conference of the United Church. While Jack attended sessions, Kathleen joined the ministers' wives group and sampled the Canadian specialties of cantaloupe sundae and pumpkin pie. Esther Gaudin showed her around the city and the two women found they had much in common. A shopping spree with Jack for a cedar chest, a year's supply of food and household goods, an organ, a canoe and six hens capped "an exceedingly kind week," in Kathleen's words.

From the conference, they rushed by taxi to Selkirk to catch the season's first run of the steamer, *The Wolverine*. They sat like royalty on the upper deck with two prospectors, looking back at their zigzag path in the sunset as they progressed up the Red River to Lake Winnipeg. The 250 miles to Warren's Landing took one and one-half days. At the fishing village on Snake Island, Kathleen met the aboriginal postmistress who had eleven children, and a 90-year-

84

old man who was the postcard image of a North American Indian yet claimed to be the first white man on the lake. The hens came through by laying two eggs which the ship's cook was glad to get. At a difficult, rocky channel near the Berens River reserve, wooden crosses marked the spot where a missionary couple, their four children and two aboriginal guides had drowned.

At Warren's Landing they transferred to a smaller steamboat, which avoided rocks and islands in the pale-green waters of Playgreen River and Lake for three-and-one-half hours. Jack and Kathleen stayed at the Gaudins' while waiting in Norway House for their freight to arrive and the winds to change. The Indian agent, the RCMP officer, the principal and the whole teaching staff of the school invited them for meals. At the hospital, the doctor went over their medical supplies and taught Jack how to give injections and pull teeth. For forty very difficult years Anna Gaudin had given the aboriginals first aid and nursing care. She had lost three infant daughters and an infant son to disease.

By six a.m. on June 11, 1928 two 16-foot canvas canoes, equipped with oars and sails as well as paddles, were packed and ready. The school launch offered them a tow over to Hope Island and Kathleen and Jack got in. They had not gone many yards when one canoe started going in all directions because of the unbalanced load. All of Kathleen's belongings were on the verge of dumping. Jack's friends and guides, Isaac Mason and Geordie Grieves, jumped into the water and, after a struggle, managed to climb into the canoe and sail it. After having tea at Monkmans' on the island, they departed with a care package of oranges, cream and eggs.

The two transporters shoved off in the freight canoe first, sailing eastward along the Nelson River to Sea Falls, Hairy Lake (named for the reeds sticking out of it), the Echimamish River, the Height of Land and Robinson Portage, where they would wait up. This route had been plied by HBC York boats up until 1923 and the wooden railway formerly used to roll the boats over the portage was still there. Many centuries ago, a group of Cree had separated from the main Algonquin tribe on the east coast of the continent. Driven west by famine, they came to the prairies where they encountered hostile Sioux. The Cree fled in birch bark canoes to get away from their enemies, who did not have as good canoes, and opened up the whole territory from Ontario to the Rocky Mountains.

The second canoe had Geordie in the bow, the crate of hens behind him, Kathleen and Jack facing the hens and Isaac in the stern. Luggage was stuffed in between them. They sailed, shot small rapids, stopped at Sea Falls Portage and crossed stepping-stones to find a place to eat (and, in Kathleen's case, change out of her skirt.) Farther on, at Hairy Lake, they saw three canoes from God's Lake. The sail jibed and came off the mast in the strong wind but the men got it back on. They stopped at the mouth of the Echimamish for tea, then went on and pitched their tent on spongy soil at 8 p.m. They had come forty-five miles.

Kathleen woke early to the sound of pounding rain but it stopped by 8 a.m. and they rowed out into a pretty world. The dark waters of the narrow river were overhung by thick willows which brushed against her and gave her a shut-in feeling, as if there were no life around. Then they came to an opening at some small, impassable rapids. When the men tried to pull the canoe through by getting out and standing on rocks, Isaac fell in and got wet. They stopped for lunch early and built a fire so he could dry out. The northern scenery of rapids, rocks and towering trees was captivating Kathleen. A chorus of frogs accompanied them past marshlands with low bushes and fir trees beyond. The sun shone, the wind blew and the river broadened. At a shallow stretch the oars struck mud and the canoe grounded. Jack helped get it going by walking and paddling.

A forest fire had ravished the land around and a submerged rock ripped a hole in the bottom of the canoe, causing it to leak slightly. At a spot where they had to get out and walk, Kathleen slipped and sat in the water so had to change in the bush. They battled upstream against a head-wind and adverse current until they rested and drank tea at 2:30 p.m. In the next hour they reached the Height of Land, where they portaged to another creek which flowed downstream into a wider river. Kathleen faced into a cold, north wind as the hens pecked at her straw hat from behind. After logging forty more miles that day, they struck camp, had supper, said their prayers and went to sleep.

The men began to stir at 3:30 a. m.; it hardly got dark at all at this time of year. They set off at 5:30 a.m. and were hailed by a Swedish trapper in another canoe who called out to Jack, "You're going to get it! You're late!" They reached Robinson Portage at 6:15

a.m. to find the two transporters who had gone ahead asleep on the beach. They had pushed their canoe and the freight over the portage in the wooden railway's two steel-wheeled carriages. Kathleen could hear the rushing sound of Robinson Falls, a long stretch of rapids, but didn't go over to see them because of the wet grass and mosquitoes. Jack helped her walk over the slippery, two-mile portage while the men pulled the second canoe-load up the steep incline, then restrained it on the way down. By 7:45 a.m. the two canoes were reloaded and sailing along the 12-mile extent of Robinson Lake in a fair wind. They stopped for meals whenever Isaac got hungry and today lunch was at 10 a.m.

After they started sailing again, they encountered the Oxford House chief and his son, who were taking a sick man by canoe to the Norway House Hospital. Around noon the missionary's party reached High Hill portage, a steep hill over a mile high. They carried their belongings over, reloaded and shoved off again in only one and one-quarter hours. Now they headed northeast into Moriah Lake, famous for its echoing cliffs. They stopped for tea before entering Pine Lake because a strong wind and dark clouds overhead looked very threatening. They could see rough waves ahead as they lingered in the small river. The skies burst suddenly so they took cover under their macintoshes during a ten-minute inundation. Now Windy Lake calmed down and they sailed steadily ahead until they encountered a head-wind. Then they camped for the night in the shelter of a sharp point.

Next morning, on the other side of Windy Lake, they arrived at the gorgeous rapids in the little river feeding into Oxford Lake, where blue waters plummeted over mossy green stones. They shot some of the rapids and portaged others as huge Jackfish swam in front of the tall, green trees. They were reloading at the last portage, Waypinahpanns, when two canoes landed. It was a Cree custom to paddle out to greet new arrivals. The Oxford House men shook hands solemnly with Kathleen and then, just as solemnly, with Isaac and Geordie, whom they had known all their lives. How she was amused and savored her new freedom! In English society, so many little things, such as shaking hands with a person you had already met, simply 'were not done'.

At 9:30 a.m. they entered 40-mile-long Oxford Lake and sailed at such a thrilling pace that Kathleen's hat box flew overboard. Geordie retrieved the tennis balls, oranges and other odds and ends. At 3 p.m. they caught the first glimpse of the rock outcroppings at Oxford House, altitude 700 ft. At 4:45 p.m. they stopped on a rocky island to tidy up and at 6 p.m. they arrived.

The Indian chief, many of the reserve's 400 members and Nelson were standing on shore to greet them. Kathleen felt shy but, in no time, Jack had her on her feet, out of the canoe and shaking hands. They walked up the path and he carried her over the threshold of *Mission House*. Before they could finish eating supper, the two HBC clerks and then the factors dropped in. Mrs. Davidson had come out from Scotland as a bride a year ago and had found her winter as the only white woman on the reserve difficult. She had just returned from a visit to the doctor and a prolonged rest in Winnipeg. The McIvors also came by. After they left, Kathleen and Jack lingered in the doorway looking at the display made by a distant forest fire.

Kathleen saw the other Oxford House women going out to their fishing nets every day and setting rabbit snares in the bush. When the hunters came in with moose hides the women scraped them in a frame and tanned them by the fire. They made them into beautifully embroidered moccasins, slippers, mitts and parkas which were snapped up by tourists in Norway House. The women dried strips of moose and deer meat to make *pemmican* (dried meat pounded and made into cakes with fat and dried berries) and they threaded fish on sticks to smoke them for winter dog food.

The women dressed in the 18th-century style of shawls and long skirts which the Scottish Hudson Bay factors' wives had worn. They were the first persons to come here bearing bibles and practicing the habits of praying and hymn singing. Not ones to be left behind in the world of fashion, the older girls and some of the young wives cut off their lovely long black hair to make it look like Kathleen's. To her surprise, she was a teen-age idol!

On her first Sunday in the Oxford House church, the beauty of the Cree language impressed Kathleen as Isaac read the scriptures. Jack read the same passage in English and the hymns were sung in both languages at once. She thought of the text that had inspired her to devote her life to mission work: "Other sheep have I and they too must be brought into the fold." [John 10:16].

90

The British Wesleyan Methodists had been invited by the HBC to open the Norway House mission in 1840. Its labor force was being sucked south of the border by the magical appeal of circuit preachers and the Bible. The Rev. James Evans, who wore a buckskin jacket and long hair, spawned a movement of charismatic aboriginal preachers in northern Manitoba. He invented a syllabic alphabet and taught it by carving the characters into a birch tree. The nine characters, when each is turned four ways, stand for the thirty-six sounds they use. This language still unites the Cree people, who have a very high rate of literacy. The Cree hymnbook printed by Evans in 1841 was the first book printed in western Canada. A Cree copy of St. John's Gospel and other passages of the Bible soon followed. The materials he used were clay, sturgeon oil, chimney soot, lead foil from the lining of tea chests and a leather-press.

The story goes that Evans opposed the HBC for making aboriginal employees work on Sundays. He also condemned the head factor for choosing a woman for himself from among the wives of each chief in the area. The HBC opposed Evans' interference by accusing him of having sexually molested a sick woman, an allegation difficult to refute in a court where the head factor was also the judge. Just then, Evans accidentally killed a close aboriginal associate while placing a loaded rifle into a canoe. He was sent home to England and died of a heart attack almost immediately, at age forty-five.

Years later, an Oxford House woman confessed on her deathbed that she had been bribed to make the accusation of sexual

91

molestation against Evans. His Ojibway assistant Rev. H. B. Steinhauer established a resident mission at Oxford House in 1851 and the reserve converted to Christianity in 1900. The ashes of Evans, a hero to the Cree people, were buried in a ceremony at Norway House in 1955.

Settling into married life, Kathleen sewed curtains on her treadle machine while Jack planted seeds. They and Nelson shared the two-bedroom bungalow, finished with beautiful hardwood floors and white siding which the church provided. Most of the people lived cramped up in teepees or shacks. The mission team organized a field day for the last day of school with events such as climbing the pole, threading the needle and scrambling for sweets.

One of the first callers was Napao Munroe, who wanted advice on what to name his baby. Names were very important; they indicated a connection with another person which might be helpful in times of need. After listening to suggestions, he decided to call his son Walter, the first name of Kathleen's father, and Gordon, the surname of the Indian agent. The christening ceremony gave Kathleen an occasion to use some of her silver and lace wedding presents. At least a dozen people came every day to barter food, get first aid or other help, ask advice, arrange a baptism or wedding or have a tooth pulled. Kathleen discovered that the aboriginal remedy of wet tea leaves worked on burns.

Two of her favorite callers were the Curleyheads. Alice always managed to charm a little extra out of Jack in the way of supplies. David had lost the use of both legs, due to arthritis, so had to sit down and push himself along with both arms. When he was young, he had been stranded alone for six weeks on an island. He had his Cree hymnbook with him so memorized all the hymns and never lost hope he would be saved. He kept himself alive by eating seagulls' eggs. Another favorite was Bobbie Chubb, who liked to brag. He told Kathleen he disciplined his children by locking the door of his house at 10 p.m. every night. Then he looked at his watch and said, "Tonight I have locked myself out."

Seventy families (147 church members) were in Jack's pastoral care. In the past year he had had eight baptisms, three weddings and ten funerals. His annual salary was $1297 from the Church, plus $50 from the Government for serving as medical dispenser. Kathleen balanced the books of the mission, one of the church's most successful. By accounting for every last tablespoonful of flour she reported a surplus of seventy-two cents.

On the way back from a baby's funeral with a coffin in the canoe, Kathleen and Jack tossed their wolf/husky dog, Byng, into the water because of his disrespectful panting.

Kathleen was trying to figure out how to fillet a trout as smoke from the distant forest fire wafted in through the kitchen window. Just then Jack spotted two canoe-loads of visitors far up the lake so he ran and got Eva Bell, his Cree housekeeper, to help Kathleen. Fish and potatoes were prepared, scones baked, beds made up and oranges and milk set out on the dining room table by the time the canoes arrived.

They contained the missionary couple from God's Lake and their two daughters, a couple with a baby, and two prospectors. One of the latter had a pair of lynx pups he was planning to sell to the Winnipeg zoo. The prospectors' canoe had an engine on it and was towing the other one. Two mining instructors from the University of Toronto were already sleeping on the verandah but they moved out into a tent with Nelson as Kathleen shuffled things around until everyone had a place. She and Jack slept on the floor. Fourteen people sat down for breakfast at 7 a.m. before the guests took to their canoes again.

The forest fire got worse and advanced closer. Kathleen stayed home from church, because of a bilious attack, but was roused from her bed by the sound of the fire. It was terribly frightening to see great volumes of smoke rising into the air. Across the river, flames were leaping high and licking the tops of the evergreens. They caught fire, burned brightly for a few moments and fell off.

Practically all of northern Manitoba was on fire. An aboriginal forestry ranger commandeered 100 prospectors and trappers to fight the fire in the Island Lake district, then flew up to Oxford House and directed a group of men all night. The danger was not so much from the fire across the river as from one behind them at Back Lake. The pilot said he would fly up there to check it out and drop a note on his way back if they were in danger. Meanwhile, the men rescued the people who lived on the other side of the river and prevented the fire from leaping across. The wind changed and the pilot dropped nothing when he flew over, to everyone's huge relief.

Near the beginning of August, the hunters, trappers, transporters, guides and other workers belonging to the Oxford House band returned home. Since the white man frowned on dancing and pagan beliefs, treaty time replaced the traditional ceremonies held to seek the totem god's protection and blessing. When the plane carrying Dr. Turpel and Indian agent Gordon arrived, things got underway. The doctor examined the people, pulled teeth, prescribed medicine and vaccinated everyone against smallpox. Jack accompanied him and received instructions on how to follow up with certain cases. Kathleen visited the women who were sick and a teen-age girl who had had a stillborn baby, the 'farewell present' of the HBC clerk who had been transferred the previous fall.

With Mr. Gordon presiding, the men elected their chief and two councilors. All male members of the tribe sat in council to decide questions, big and small, and serve as a court. Jack had been trying to persuade the people not to re-elect the same chief year after year but to no avail. It was a very heavy job. This year the elections had to be held twice because the chief was sick and resigned after one day. Mr. Gordon handed out the government annuity of $5 to each person and spoke in church on treaty Sunday.

After the treaty party flew off, a heap of big bags and boxes appeared on the grassy green and the Cree gathered around them in family groups with their baskets and containers. The chief, the councilors and other prominent men each took a sack of sugar, flour, etc. and went around the circle measuring the food out a cupful at a time. When the long, drawn-out ceremony was over, they feasted and danced until late into the night. Treaty week was jammed full with weddings and baptisms. Jack thought this time of jollification was good for the people, with everyone able to buy trinkets that caught the eye and stirred the imagination. Kathleen watched the men buy new sweaters which they pulled over their old ones for added warmth. She counted how many they were wearing by looking at the colors showing through the holes.

As the treaty party was preparing to leave the reserve, Kathleen drew Dr. Turpel aside and told him she had not had any regular menstrual periods since she came to Canada. Now she was getting a 'bloody show' (medical terminology) from time to time. He said she might be pregnant or her symptoms might be due to the radical changes she had made in country and lifestyle. If her symptoms got worse, she should come down to the hospital to see him.

Big Lad, Kathleen and children try out the cariole as her due date nears

10. The Cariole Ride

The bleeding continued so Jack, Isaac and Jimmy took
Kathleen by canoe to the Norway House hospital in early September.
Dr. Turpel examined her and said she was expecting a baby but there
was a danger of a miscarriage. Luckily, the prone position in the
canoe for five days had been the best thing for her. The doctor
prescribed another ten days' bed rest in the hospital and the trouble
cleared up completely. An airplane was flying up to Oxford House
so Kathleen was able to send a message to Jack, saying she was well
enough to return. If it wasn't too late for him to come down, they
wouldn't have to spend the winter apart. Jack and his two guides
promptly jumped into a canoe.

On the way home, Isaac misjudged the force of the wind out
on Oxford Lake and yelled "We're not going to make it!" while

Jimmy thumped his chest and said "My heart's going like this!" Somehow they overpowered the waves, got the canoe under control and made it to shore, almost completely swamped with water. Soaking wet, they got going again. As they pulled into Oxford House on September 27th the first big snowstorm of the season, and of Kathleen's life, was in close pursuit. Jack bought her a wolf skin for $25 to keep her warm.

A father of two small children fell through the ice and drowned in October and an outbreak of chicken pox afflicted the reserve. Kathleen and Jack had no party to celebrate their first anniversary. After the epidemic abated, the McIvors and Davidsons came over to listen to radio concerts. Wilson, Jack's brother, arrived and helped with the church services, wood-hauling and last of the haying. It was his first trip away from Ontario and, on the trail in, a red beard emerged to mock his blond hair. He brought letters containing news of Eric's wedding and of King George V's illness. Kathleen formed the Oxford House Girls' Club and taught them how to sing together as a choir for the Christmas concert.

She thought it would be best for their baby if it were born in a hospital, with a doctor attending, and Jack agreed this was a sensible idea. Among the texts he chose for his sermons were "Be ye not over-anxious "[Matthew 6:34] and "The woman with the issue of blood" [Luke 8:43]. They had to get out safely before her due date in the depth of the deep winter freeze but, in the meantime, the Christmas season was looming. She was in good health but he was haunted by an experience he had had when he was a student minister

98

at Warren's Landing. The doctor had asked him to help take a pregnant, young Cree woman who was suffering from toxemia to hospital. She was screaming from pain and so delirious she had to be restrained. They did not get there in time to save her.

Jack hitched Big Lad up to the cariole to pull Kathleen over to the Davidsons' at the HBC for tea.   This type of snow sled was perfected by ancient aboriginals in Alaska who called it a *nobugidaban*, the root of the word toboggan.[1] It is made of thin hardwood boards, curved up at one end using heat or steam. Cleats of wood are attached across the boards to hold them together. They are also fastened along the sides, providing side-rails through which a cord can be passed back and forth to secure the load. Another cord is attached to the upturned front for pulling over the snow by dogs. In the 19th century, the French Canadians used a similar conveyance, pulled by either a horse or dogs, and called it a cariole.

Unfortunately, after the excursion Kathleen came down with a terrible cold. She was unable to help with the Christmas concert and Mrs. Davidson had to replace her as organist on Christmas Sunday. All the hunters came in from their winter camps to trade their furs and attend the Christmas church service. Afterwards, Jack was happily surprised to find Kathleen up on her feet and simmering one of the hens (two of them had been eaten by dogs) on the stove. Later that day, Jack married the widow of the former chief, who had just died, to the new chief. The HBC clerks, Stanley and Henry,

---

[1] "Snow Travel in Ancient Canada", Ian Dyck of the Canadian Museum of Civilization

came for dinner on New Year's Day to eat a rooster Stanley's father had sent up from Norway House.

Father persuaded Regan Munroe, the young man he had married on short notice the summer before, not to go back to the hunt but to be their guide for the trip. Jack Gordon, the Indian agent's son who succeeded Nelson as school-teacher, agreed to look after the work of the mission while they were away. The deal was that Jack would lend him Tommy and the cariole to take to Norway House to spend the holidays with his parents. After he got back, Tommy would need a few days' rest before Kathleen and Jack set out.

Tommy sensed his master was feeding and patting him especially attentively, examining his harness and the cariole with extra care. He knew he was going to be entrusted to do something only an exceptional horse like himself could do and he would give it his all. Kathleen was getting excited about the prospect of dashing through the snow in a one-horse open sleigh, even though Tommy didn't have bells or a bob-tail.

It was -30 F on the morning of Jan. 15, 1929 when Kathleen emerged from Mission House, after spending more time choosing her wardrobe and dressing than she had for any Mayor's ball or Royal event. She was wearing her fur coat, now with a big hood attached, a pair of Jack's breeches and a pair of winter moccasins. Pieces of eiderdown, her own invention, were folded around her ankles in the shape of feet. Underneath, her delicate condition's first layer of fortification against the cold was a set of long, combination underwear. On top of this, she wore a sweater, a pair of Jack's long, woolen pants and two pairs of heavy socks. Her hands and forearms were covered with the Indian gauntlets Mr. Gordon had given her as a hostess present at treaty time. In short, she was very sensibly dressed for what lay ahead.

Jack put his finishing touch on the loaded cariole and helped Kathleen into her first-class accommodations. The big toboggan was 8' 2" long and 2' 3" wide; it had a wooden back rest about two-thirds of the way along its length and a wooden frame to hold up its canvas sides. Behind the back rest, Jack placed a bag of oats for Tommy, a grub box containing enough food for three people for six days and a jerry (chamber-pot) discreetly concealed in a sack. On the cariole itself, he had carefully arranged Regan's bag of clothes and blanket, his own and Kathleen's two small kit bags, a box and a suitcase. All this was covered with an ample mattress of hay. Jack tucked Kathleen in with a huge, khaki, canvas-covered eiderdown underneath her and another one on top.

The trip had been delayed for several days, due to blowing snow, but now the weather had cleared and the sun was shining. The route to the hospital, 180 miles to the southwest (twenty miles shorter than in summer) lay mainly over rivers and lakes frozen several feet deep with a layer of snow on top. Kathleen sat semi-reclined on top of the load, while Jack jogged alongside holding Tommy's reins and Regan ran ahead to blaze the trail.

Basic to Kathleen's comfort was the fact that, from her vantage point, Jack was always in sight. She was madly in love with him, had complete faith in him and would follow him anywhere. He was "awfully good to her and wonderfully strong and fit in both wind and limb" (quotes from her journal.) She had with her a rubber hot-water bottle and some chocolates, just in case she should have to give birth prematurely along the way. As they got going, one of her eyelashes froze to the fur trim on her hood and she watched Jack's face frame with rime formed by his moist, warm breath landing on his collar and cap.

Twenty minutes out, they stopped to say goodbye to Dulas and Alice McIvor at their store on the Point. She had become Kathleen's best friend and was very concerned about her. Cree women had more sense than to venture out on long trips in winter. They gave birth to their babies in a tepee with a midwife attending. Kathleen did not stir from her embalmment in the cariole, so Alice came out to wish her well before they went on.

At mid-day, the toboggan party found shelter by the side of Oxford Lake, gathered wood, built a huge fire and unpacked the grub box of its contents: two frying pans, two tea pails and frozen food. The whole glob of cooked meat, beans, bread and butter was dumped into the frying pan to thaw out and heat through. Kathleen had never eaten out in the cold before and was hungry. No sooner had she put the steel fork into her mouth than it froze and tore away the skin, making her lip bleed.

They traveled on but by sundown were still out on Oxford Lake so camped on shore around 5 p.m. After their meal, Kathleen tried to go to sleep in the cariole but woke up every hour feeling cramped. The fire roasted her on one side while she froze on the other, so she had to keep constantly revolving. Jack and Regan made themselves beds of spruce boughs on the ground and rolled up in their bedding. Regan slept soundly in his single blanket but Jack not a wink in his eiderdown. Well-blanketed, Tommy stood watch, tied to a tree under the starry sky amid the softly sighing spruces. A nose-bag prevented him from wasting even one of his precious oats and he had eaten his nightly ration of hay from Kathleen's mattress. Over the past three winters, he had taken Jack over 750 square miles of territory to visit isolated camps, spending over twenty nights wide-awake like this in the open.

Jack got the fire going at 3 a.m. and at 5 a.m. they ate breakfast. Kathleen promptly threw up and blamed all the rotating between heat and cold for the loss. They pushed on and crossed three small portages around rapids, which let Kathleen ease her backbone and stretch her legs. These narrow bush paths were more sheltered than the open trail. After camping at mid-day, she felt ill and miserable all afternoon, being sore, cold and shaken by the motion. Her mattress was getting thinner as they progressed! They went over more portages of one-half mile or so in length from lake to lake.

By the time they stumbled into the log house "of no great dimensions"(words from Kathleen's journal) owned by the Chubbs on Pine Lake, it seemed like heaven to her. It had an outer living room with an open fireplace ventilated by a hole in the roof. That night all seven of the Cree—Bobbie, his wife, two sons, two daughters and Regan—slept on the floor, while their guests were given the inner room, which had a stove and a built-in bed. Kathleen felt pretty sick and they contemplated staying for one or two days. However, after a good night's sleep she was feeling fairly fit, so they parted from their cheery hosts.

They pushed on all day and stopped just for meals. By now Kathleen had got her trail legs but was stiff from lying so long in the same position and had a sore end to her spine. Towards evening, they walked the four-mile length of Robinson portage and, after sunset, struck an empty old shack. It was low and drafty but "four walls and a roof are something to be grateful for even if you do hit your head every time you stand up," she wrote later. They lit the dilapidated stove but had forgotten to bring candles. It was cold sleeping on the floor but Kathleen's fur coat kept her warm. Jack didn't have a fur coat, let alone eiderdown foot wrappings, and suffered.

After an early start the next day, they reached a Cree winter camp at noon. Having dinner, resting and warming herself in a very clean house put Kathleen on a high. She felt so good she gave one of her chocolates to each of the five children scampering about. That night, Regan led the cariole party to the cabin of John Kirkness, a hermit who lived miles away from anyone on Molson Lake. Part aboriginal and part white, he was well educated, had served in the war and had worked in lumber camps. His wall was decorated with a home-made calendar and recipes for pie. He, too, had no candles so he put melted butter in a saucer with a piece of cloth to give light. That night, Kathleen and the three men all slept on the floor of the one room. Jack's help at a little undressing underneath their eiderdown made it ripple mysteriously.

They rose before sunrise to face a big dip in the temperature and sixty miles yet to go. Not far out on the lake, Jack's nose and chin froze and Kathleen was horrified, expecting them to drop off. He explained that this was not unusual in the north, the spots would go white and then develop into a blister and sore, like a bad sunburn. When they got to Charlie Saunders' house, the last on the trail, they thawed themselves out and ate. Not wanting to spend another night in the open, they pushed on. They camped briefly around 6:30 p.m. at a point with tall trees and plenty of dry wood where they could build a fire and eat grub.

Regan carried a fire-bag of embers from stop to stop so he could get the fire going quickly. On a night such as this in January, 1841, Evans had written in his diary, "Water from a kettle nearly boiling, poured into a tin plate to a depth of about one-half inch, becomes frozen in one-and-one-half minutes at -42 F." The cariole party didn't have a thermometer and didn't have time to do experiments. They just drank three or four cups of tea which magically stayed warm and invigorated them. At 10 p.m. they stopped again to rest Tommy, and Kathleen managed to sleep for over an hour.

At midnight, they rested at the portage between the Muscataban and Nelson rivers and lit a fire, supervised by the crescent moon. Out again on the trail at 2:30 a.m., it suddenly became dark and they got lost. This had happened a few times before but Regan always found the way by stopping the procession and walking a few paces, first in one direction, then in each of the others. He studied the snow, the vegetation, the trees, the wind and the skies for signs. Then he sat down to think until he figured out which way to go. This is what he did now, while his charges sat silently waiting for guidance, with Jack fingering his pocket compass.

Regan got them back onto the trail but four miles out from Norway House one side of the cariole broke. This added to Kathleen's discomfort on what little was left of the hay mattress. The toboggan limped onward and finally reached its destination at 4 a.m. on Sunday, Jan. 20. The night-duty nurse opened the door of the hospital and let them in. Seeing Kathleen's condition, she listened for the fetus' heartbeat and it came through loud and strong. The baby had ridden comfortably and well protected in its caul. Kathleen and Jack were dead beat and too strung up to sleep but immensely relieved. Jack was exhausted, having walked most of the way; Kathleen was severely constipated but otherwise in the pink of condition. Regan was fine. Poor scruffy-looking little Tommy, a genuine hero in disguise, was almost played out. Later that morning, Jack went to church and Kathleen wrote home.

They were safe now and sure that everything was going to be all right. For the four days and five nights of the cariole ride they had been practical people preoccupied by anxiety but now the truth sank in on Kathleen and Jack. They were immersed in ecstasy, at least as far as their natures would allow! The sparkling heavens, the white snow blanketing the earth, the silent vastness and the bowing trees transformed the whole universe into an awesome cathedral. Like actors in a Christmas pageant, they had thought only of getting to the place where the baby would be born. They had ventured forth, putting themselves in God's care alongside the other most humble and fearsome creatures. They had prepared for the trip and kept their attitude correct, asking for guidance and proceeding one day at a time.

Kathleen was Jack's lady and he was her knight, the heroine and hero of an epic story. The cariole ride bonded them on a deeper level of existence and kept them going for the rest of their lives. The risks he took, the comfort and familiarity she abandoned, the challenges and hardships they weathered all reached a climax on this day. But as a celebration of the birth of their child, their feelings were premature.

A party was held for all the babies born on the reserve that year

11. Hello to a New Life

Jack had to get back to work but would return when the baby
was due. After a week's rest, he set out with Regan and Tommy.
Moccasin telegrams (notes handed to travelers encountered on the
trail) kept Kathleen informed of his progress. He had a good sleep at
the Saunders' on Tuesday, reached the Chubbs' on Friday and
expected to be home on Saturday, in plenty of time to get his sermon
ready for Sunday.

When Jack got up Saturday morning, anxious to hit the trail,
he went out to hitch Tommy up but he wasn't there. Jack thought he
must have just wandered off and would be waiting for him and
Regan, pawing for grass underneath the snow. Bobbie offered to take
them as far as his fish cache on his sleigh but the horse was nowhere
in sight.

In fact, Tommy was far away, free of the cariole at last, heading full tilt for his stable. When the horse galloped into Oxford House all by himself, with no sign of the cariole or human life, the people were very upset. The hours passed with still no sign of Jack and Regan and the people's concerns grew very grave. They feared the worst. Dulas organized a search party and they were just setting out at 1 a.m., Sunday, when Jack and Regan straggled in, exhausted but safe. They had walked the last sixty miles without any provisions. Jack conducted his church services that morning but came down with a bad cold which lasted for a week. Regan went back to Bobbie's on Tuesday with a dog team to fetch the cariole and luggage.

Kathleen didn't need hospital care, so she stayed with the Gaudins for two weeks and then with the Gordons. On Saturday, Feb. 23, a few days before her due date, she went for a walk in the morning, felt some discomfort in the afternoon and checked into the hospital in the evening. Dr. Turpel examined her and said all was normal; the baby would not come for a number of hours, probably not until the next morning. The waters had not yet broken. Then he went with his wife to play bridge five miles up the river.

The labor cramps started coming on stronger and closer together as midnight approached. The night-duty nurse sent a messenger up the river to get the doctor. A new life was determined to come out into the light of the world. The nurse reassured Kathleen by telling her the severe pains were necessary and instructed her gently in what to do. As the fetus began to emerge, the nurse took one look at it and exclaimed, "What on earth is this?" Kathleen wondered, "What indeed?" as the nurse turned around and fled. Since this was a real emergency, Kathleen's nerves held steady as a rock as she waited alone.

Like the hero of Charles Dickens' David Copperfield, the baby was being born in its caul. The unruptured sac of inner membranes was still covering her head and face, making them look grotesque. In English folklore, a child born in this rare manner was destined never to meet death by drowning. David Copperfield's dried-up caul was sold at auction as a good-luck charm.

Head Nurse Oliver was awakened from her sleep in another room of the hospital and now assumed control. She knew she must break open the caul immediately or else the baby would choke on amniotic fluid with its first breath. And so it was that Tanis Elizabeth Kell, a beautiful, healthy, 7 1/2 lb. baby girl, was born. She was three-quarters of an hour old when the doctor arrived and three days old when her father saw her for the first time.

Jack stayed to celebrate Kathleen's 29th birthday on March 9th and then they parted again, since it was too cold to take the baby on a trip. They would meet again in seven weeks' time when the spring waters flowed. While Kathleen and Tanis stayed with the Gordons and Gaudins, Jack returned to work. He wrote pamphlets entitled Why We Are Protestants, How to Read the Bible, The Christian Life, and What Jesus Means to Me, all of which the McIvors translated into Cree.

In late May, Jack and two guides started out for Norway House with a canoe tied onto a toboggan. The lake ice was barely thick enough for walking and the edgewater barely wide enough for paddling. They reached Hairy Lake in six days' time, on a Sunday, and found all sorts of campers sitting out in the sun. They looked like a congregation to Jack so he held a service.

After Jack was reunited with Kathleen and Tanis, they got on a private motor boat that would get them to Warren's Landing in time for *The Wolverine's* first run of the season. They were lucky they didn't drown. The boat was overloaded, almost ran out of gas and leaked so badly all the passengers had to help bail it out. After the church conference in Winnipeg ended, the family made their way home through oppressive heat and thunder storms to tackle Jack's fifth year of problematic missionary work.

Alice's gifts were a birch bark basket and trivets, and pants for Tanis

12. Goodbye to the Swampy Cree

Kathleen fitted the women and girls with coats from bales of clothing sent by southern congregations. By charging five cents for each leftover item, they made $5 to help buy siding for the church building. The Cree paid one-tenth of the cost of the mission, not including Jack's salary.

Eva, the housekeeper, was keen to marry off her 15-year-old daughter to a boy who wanted her but Kathleen persuaded Jack to try to get the groom to postpone his plans for a year. However, Eva asserted traditional Cree parental authority and Jack had to marry them. Kathleen tried to tolerate Eva's ways but, when she put Jack's white shirts on to boil with his red socks, she replaced her. One day the three cows got out when Jack was away so Kathleen ran a mile-and-a-half to get Fred Stevens, the new teacher from Toronto, who dismissed his class and rounded up the cows.

Ten horses working for Ross Navigation Company came in from Cross Lake, pulling ten flat sleighs loaded with drums of gasoline. It was enough to power every canoe in God's Lake and Oxford House and make the silent, skillful paddle a thing of the past forever. A Sikorsky containing businessmen headed for York Factory was forced down on the reserve by the weather.

On August 23rd Kathleen gave breakfast to two NAME mining company pilots, Val Patriarch and Carl Mews, and watched them fly off towards God's Lake. At dusk Val's plane returned but Carl's did not. After six days, a search party found his plane and a note saying he was walking to Oxford House, expecting to arrive in three days' time. Two expert guides, Donald Wood and Stanley Nattaway, were flown out to track him and, after nine days, narrowed the search down to within a few miles. They found Carl on September 9th, thin and with his clothes torn by bushes, but otherwise unhurt. The guides were heroes.

Freeze-up came in mid-November and silence replaced the drone of boat or plane. Since her courageous cariole trek of the previous winter, Kathleen had acquired a thermometer, parenthood and experience. The idea of other people going out and taking chances scared her stiff. One day, when it was -45 F, she got a note from Fred saying he had sent his dog team and toboggan on ahead and was walking the last day in from Cross Lake. By the time he arrived, just before midnight, she was frazzled. Another day she was expecting Bobbie, now student minister at God's Lake, but he didn't show up. He had had to turn back because two of his dogs died.

The day after Christmas, Jack and Isaac set out so they could help Bobbie with the New Year's services but they hit the wrong trail, wasted two days and came back. They started out again and Kathleen panicked when she realized they were camping out at -52 F. Actually, Jack was reading Reader's Digest by the light of his flashlight because he couldn't sleep and, as a result, he got a bad frostbite. Kathleen hadn't come to this continent to be widowed and left alone. When he got back she told him he'd better stop taking such risks!

The Cree mothers constantly fondled, hugged and kissed their babies on the mouth and Kathleen was afraid they were giving them TB. She kept Tanis in her carriage, except when they were alone, and told the people this was the white people's custom. Tanis loved it when older children leaned over the sides of her carriage to amuse her. If she cried in church, Jack stepped down from the pulpit to give her his gold fountain pen to play with.

On Tanis' first birthday, Kathleen held a party for all the babies born on the reserve that year. She baked a cake, took pictures and held a contest for the finest Oxford House baby. The chief was the judge and he chose his grandson. Tanis was adventuresome and in a single day upset her carriage, pulled a lemon pie over her head and swallowed an aspirin. Kathleen took the hint and let her out to crawl about freely. Now that she was no longer a captive Tanis soon learned to walk.

The Catholic school at Cross Lake burned down due to an over-heated stove, killing eight children and the mother superior. Many Cree believed someone who wanted this to happen had cast a spell upon them but Jack was trying to eradicate such superstition.

The hunt was lean and the mighty hunters sat brooding, wondering why they were failing, immobilized by depression.

On March 10th Donald, last September's hero, was pulled in from winter camp completely out of his mind. His friends said he had drunk lemon extract two days before but Jack suspected something worse. There was no beer on the reserve in this Prohibition era but there was home brew. He confirmed the symptoms of gasoline poisoning in his medical book. There was no antidote; the only cure was to vomit the gasoline up instantly but it was too late for that. Donald's drink had been spiked, either by pranksters or himself, but no one confessed at a meeting held to try to get at the truth of what had happened. He was doomed to develop pneumonia within a few weeks' time and die horribly.

Jack wanted to take him out to hospital by dog team, since weather conditions were excellent and Mrs. Davidson offered to supply rations for the trip. However, the first mercy flight in northern Manitoba had been flown the previous August and the chief wanted to send for an airplane. Jack said that would take longer. The assembled council asked Jack to administer communion to Donald but Jack wasn't going to pretend it was like magic. An aboriginal with traditional beliefs got better only when he took something he was convinced would make him better. Jack's interpretation of the sacrament was that a community of believers ate bread and drank wine as symbols of a commitment to live out Christ's compassion in their own lives.

A cover-up darkened this tragedy so Jack preached on the sin of lying. Next day, three guilty-looking friends of Donald asked if they could chop wood for the school. Jack visited him every day to pray and provide comfort but Donald was terrified by *wetigoes*. Then Jack preached on Elijah, who put the prophets of superstition to death. He followed up by telling the people that "the Lord reproves him whom he loves as does a father the son in whom he delights" [Proverbs 3:12]. Finally, he chose the text, "Work out your own salvation" [Philippians 2:12]. It was time for the people to train their own leaders, not be dependent on white men who came and went.

Building lumber arrived, paid for with $100 the people had raised over three years, and Easter was celebrated with spring in the air. Then came a big snow storm, cold weather and corpses from the

116

winter camps. Maggie Wemisk's baby who had been at Tanis' birthday party was one of them. After holding all the funerals and burials, including Donald's, Jack donned his old clothes and went out to haul wood and chop it up.

An Indian reserve didn't seem to be the best place to raise a family, so at the end of the winter they decided it was time to leave. Kathleen began to pack, leaving all she could for the people. Jack planted separate gardens for the chief, Isaac, the horses and cows, the school and the community. Tanis toddled along behind, wanting to help, and picked up the seeds he dropped.

As farewell presents, Alice made a birch bark sewing basket, three birch bark trivets, and (from Kathleen's left-over curtain material) a baby's travel outfit. It had elastic around the wrists and ankles, and the wide, stiff-brimmed hat was covered with netting and tied with a ribbon around the waist. Tanis could play with a small toy inside it or take it off when camp-fire smoke kept the mosquitoes away.

As she motored off on June 29, 1930 Kathleen was transfixed by this little band of first persons standing on the beach and singing, "In the sweet bye and bye, we shall meet on that beautiful shore." 'Oxford House', not 'Tomato Soup', was etched indelibly across her heart.

Looking out the missionary's window, 1929

Epilogue

Kathleen and Jack kept on working together and being best friends for nearly sixty more years, until he died in her arms at age ninety-one with a smile on his face. Not many months later she suffered a stroke and was admitted to hospital, where she passed away in her sleep at age ninety.

They left behind them seventy-two love letters, two wooden tennis racquets, a pair of embroidered white deerskin Indian princess slippers, two birch bark trivets, and a nosegay of dried, pressed Oxford House flowers—not to mention four generations of descendants.

Some people, like my parents, imagine that living on earth is a dress rehearsal for the afterlife, referred to as heaven. And I

118

wonder if those who enter that stage after having traveled in a cariole alongside a loved one, pulled by a noble beast and led by a faithful guide, throughout wintry days and starry nights under a hemispheric dome, aren't greeted by applause as thunderous as the cannons of war.

Please see page 120 for a Farewell Note from the Author

As a reader of this book, your opinion is sought after and valued. Please

Consider making it known before your strong impressions fade away. Go to

http://www.amazon.com/Kathleens-Cariole-Ride-Margaret-Virany/dp/09 69914253/ref=sr_1_1?s=books&ie=UTF8&qid=1420682591&sr =1-1&keywords=Kathleen%27s+Cariole+RIde

Then click on "10 customer reviews".

Follow the easy instructions to write your review of seventy-five words or more.

Thank you. The book-reading public send you a bouquet for

taking the time to do this.

I hope you enjoyed the book. I wrote it for you.

Margaret Kell Virany

margaret@kell.ca

120